LIVING AND WORKING IN INDIA

Some other titles from How To Books

Living and Working in Turkey

A City by City Guide to Living and Working in Australia

Emigrating to New Zealand

Going to Live in France

Going to Live and Work in Greece

A Guide to Studying and Living in Britain

Getting a Job Abroad

How To Retire Abroad

Living and Working in Hong Kong

Living and Working in the UK

Living and Working in China

Living and Working in New Zealand

Living and Working in America

Living and Working in Canada

howtobooks

Please send for a free copy of the latest catalogue:
How To Books
Spring Hill House, Spring Hill Road
Begbroke, Oxford OX5 1RX, United Kingdom
info@howtobooks.co.uk

www.howtobooks.co.uk

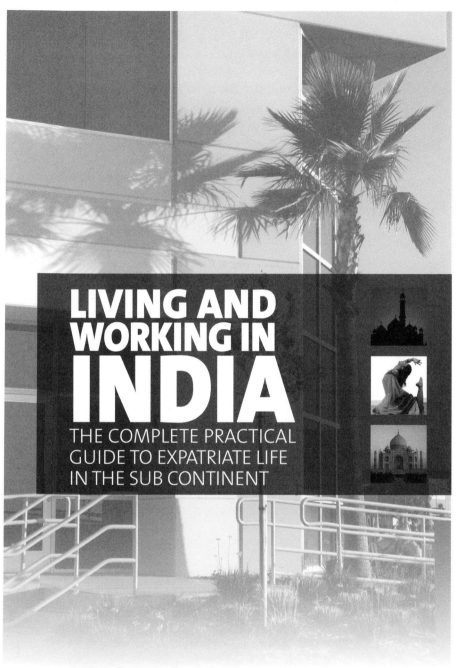

LIVING AND WORKING IN
INDIA

THE COMPLETE PRACTICAL GUIDE TO EXPATRIATE LIFE IN THE SUB CONTINENT

KRIS RAO AND
Dr IAN BEADHAM

how tobooks

ACKNOWLEDGEMENTS

We would like to express our gratitude to Rajiv Satya, Arya Hebbar, Naresh Subramaniam, Nigel Thomas, K Sivapriya, R Subramanyam, Suganthi Balakrishnan, Dr R Shankar, Sreekanth Sastry, Rev Peter Hannaway and Rev Cannon Robin Crawford for their invaluable contributions.

How To Books Ltd
Spring Hill House, Spring Hill Road
Begbroke, Oxford OX5 1RX, United Kingdom
Tel: 01865 375794 Fax: 01865 379162
info@howtobooks.co.uk
www.howtobooks.co.uk

British Library Cataloguing in Publication Data
A catalogue record for this book is available from
the British Library.

First published 2008

ISBN: 978 1 84528 199 1

Cover design by Baseline Arts Ltd, Oxford
Produced for How To Books by Deer Park Productions, Tavistock
Typeset by *specialist* publishing services ltd, Montgomery
Printed and bound by Bell & Bain Ltd, Glasgow

Contents

Preface: The Indian Experience 1

1. India's History 3
Early Civilizations 3
Advent of the Aryans 4
Dawn of Hindu Empires 5
Muslim Conquest of India 7
The Mughal Era 11
British Raj – The Jewel in the Crown 13
Indian Independence Movement 17
India 1947 to the Present Day 19

2. General Information 21
Geographical Divisions 21
The Political System 24
Religion in India 26
Languages 32
Ethnic and Cultural Divisions 34
Climate in India 36
Courts in India 38
Economy 39
Currency 40

Changing Money	40
Exchange Rates	41
Transferring and Receiving Money	41
Cash Machines and ATMs	41
Credit and Debit Cards	42
Post Office Services	42
Insurance	44
Water	44
Electricity	45
Television and DVD	45
Shopping	45
Laundry	46
Alcohol	46
Time	47
Weights and Measures	48
Telephone	48
Internet	51
Emergency Services	51
Police	52
Beggars	52
Maps	52
Gay and Lesbian Life	53
Drugs	53
Weapons	53
Public Holidays	54
Bundh (Strike)	54
Safety	55
3. Life In India	**56**
Sports	56
The Social Scene	56
'Treats' and Home Invitations	58
Expatriate Social Scene	59

Indian Films   59
Indian Music   61
The Media in India   63
Discrimination   64
Bribery and Corruption   65
Bargaining   66
Indian English   67
Indian Festivals   75
Food, Glorious Food!   77
Indian Spices   84
Indian Sweets   85

4. Immigration   86

Indian Immigration System   86
Where to Apply for Indian Visas   87
Arriving in India   90
Documents to Carry While Going to India   90
Police Registration in India   91
Where to Register   91
Registration Process   93
Documents Required   94
Residence Permit   95
Change of Details/Lost Registration   95
Lost Passport and Exit Permit   96
Late Registration   96
Extending Your Visa in India   96
Bringing in Your Dependants   97
Overstaying of Visa   97
Restricted/Protected Area Permits   98
Customs Regulations   98
Contacting your Embassy for Help   99

5. Travel 100

Travel to India 100
Getting Around in India 102
Driving 102
Public Transport 104
Travel Agencies 113

6. Employment in India 114

Recruitment 114
Employers 115
Newspapers 115
Internet Sites 115
Applying for a Job 116
The Interview 117
Work Permits or Restrictions 118
Work Environment 118
Employment Contract 122
Salaries 122
Employee Benefits 123
Equal Opportunity 123
Taxes in India 124
Income Tax Permanent Account Number 125
Working Hours 127
Paid Holidays and Time Off 127
Work Experience, Internships and Volunteer Programmes 127

7. Business in India 130

Red Tape 130
Consultancy Companies 131
Types of Business Entities 132
Taxes in India 133
Networking Organizations 135

8. Money — 137

Bringing Money to India	137
Money Transfer to India	137
Banks in India	138
Income Tax Permanent Account Number (PAN)	143
Credit Cards and Personal Loans	143

9. Housing — 144

Finding a Place	144
Rent and Deposit	147
Electricity and Water Problems	148
Bringing your Household Goods into India	149
Furnishing the House	149
Utilities	152
Newspapers	153
Domestic Services	153
Buying Property in India	156

10. Health — 159

Health Care in India	159
Indian Health System	160
Medical Facilities	161
Counselling	161
Vaccinations Required	161
Dentists	162
Pharmacies	162
Opticians	162
Health Insurance	163
Health Issues in India	163
Ayurveda	164
Other Systems of Medicines	165
Medical Tourism in India	165

11. Education   167

Education in India   167
India's Reservation System   168
Schools   169
Pre-University Colleges   171
Graduate Education   171
Admissions   172
Centres of Excellence   172

12. Leaving India   174

Before You Leave   175
Exit Permits   175
Tax Clearance Certificate   176
Changing Your Money   177
Sending Goods Back Home   177

Appendices   181

Index   212

Preface:
The Indian Experience

In recent years there has been a vast increase in the number of people who go to India, not for a holiday, but to live and work in a fascinating country that is emerging as a major world economy. This book is a product of our visit to India in 2001 when we travelled there for work.

The reasons for working in India are manifold and worth reviewing. Although your initial salary may be a little lower than it would be in the West, you can often start work in India at a higher position of responsibility and quickly gain valuable corporate experience. Moreover, while your starting salary may be lower than in a Western company, it might well translate to a higher purchasing power and standard of living. One must also remember that wages in India are increasing, while in some professions in the West, salaries are actually decreasing in real terms. And while some Indian cities are still developing in terms of amenities, you will frequently find that Indian companies often have better facilities than those you are used to in the West!

On a cultural level, nothing can quite match the vitality and sheer human experience of living in India. India's cities are lively, colourful and vibrant – although it may take a few weeks to get adjusted. Shops stay open late and there is no shortage of manpower for household services. Because English is widely used in newspapers, books, radio stations and television, your cultural transition may be easier than in other countries.

Indians are a friendly and gregarious people who are more than willing to learn about other nationalities and cultures and so you will never be short of company. If you are interested in history or archaeology, India will provide you with a live museum. Indian civilization dates back thousands of years and each empire or conqueror has left a unique historical imprint. This means that ancient Hindu shrines co-exist with Islamic-influenced Mughal architecture, imposing gateway arches from the British Raj and modern buildings. India is also a world leader in terms of music, cinema, literature, mythology and religion, so the depth of your cultural experience is practically limitless.

In addition, the friendships and connections that you form while working in India can make even a short stay there a life-changing experience. In fact, once India gets 'under your skin', you will find yourself returning to the subcontinent again and again or even settling there. The easy-going nature and warmth of the Indian people is as hard to resist as the spicy Indian cuisine, and you may soon find the sedate pace of life in the West hard to re-adjust to. Don't be surprised if you return home with a wistful longing for India and start to feel confused about which country you really call home!

Living and Working in India will ease the transition between Western and Indian cultures, giving a wealth of advice in terms of language, culture, lifestyle, education, health, housing, working practices and regulations. We hope you find this guidebook useful for both the preparation of your visit to India and throughout your stay. All the best!

Cancervive

We have committed to donate the entire proceeds of royalties from this book to Cancervive, India, a small regional charity based in Mangalore. Cancervive, India provides care and support to children with terminal cancer at hospitals around the Mangalore district.

1
India's History

To understand a country's present, one must understand its evolution over centuries. To understand India and appreciate its rich heritage, one must study its growth over time. The traditional Hindu belief is that India is a timeless country, while some modern Indian nationalists boast that it is 10,000 years old.

Even if a good part of the Indian claim is mythical, many scholars agree that it is a country with perhaps the oldest cultural and religious tradition. Many complex questions about India can only be understood by looking at its past:

- What are the religious and social divisions?
- What is the origin of the Hindu-Muslim conflict?
- Why is India so receptive to democracy?

India has one of the longest and richest histories of any country in the world. Archaeological evidence is now emerging that a civilization existed off the northwest coast of India while Europe was emerging from the Ice Age. Details of this settlement are still shrouded in myth, especially as the Hindu community and nationalist politicians have associated it with the ancient kingdom of the god Krishna that was swallowed up by the waves, like Atlantis.

EARLY CIVILIZATIONS

Leaving aside these tantalizing glimpses of cities that may be 7–10,000 years old, evidence discovered in the 1940s showed that approximately

4,500 years ago ancient cities with advanced sewerage systems were established along the River Indus in what is now Pakistan, and many artefacts of pottery and metalware have been found there.

Commonly known in the West as 'The Indus Valley Civilization', several sites have been excavated, but the best-known are at Harappa Munja (this ancient civilization is sometimes referred to as 'Harappan') and Mohenjo Daro, meaning 'mound of the dead', because of a much later Buddhist *Stupa* (monument) near the site. Archaeological evidence from pottery in the southern Indian state of Tamil Nadu suggests that civilization may have spread more widely across India at this time. Pockets of language related to the southern Indian family of languages now found in the north of India could be vestiges of a civilization that spanned India thousands of years ago.

The history of this ancient period is still emerging, and once the characters inscribed on over 1,800 traders' stamps can be deciphered, our understanding may be better. These traders' stamps were from the Indus civilization, and were known as 'the soft stone seals', as they were pressed into soft clay to leave an imprint.

ADVENT OF THE ARYANS

The next important event in ancient Indian history, around the time of the collapse of the Indus civilization some 4,000 years ago, was the appearance of a different culture in northern India; that of the Aryans. This is frequently referred to as the Aryan 'migration' to India over what is now the Khyber Pass. Another popular term is 'Aryan invasion', However, this terminology can be politically provocative, as some people associate Brahmins, who are sometimes of a paler skin colour, with invaders from the northwest. Other castes may sometimes regard themselves as 'indigenous Indians' or 'true Indians'. In fact genetic evidence has failed to corroborate the Aryan invasion hypothesis. If a civilization entered India 4,000 years ago, all that remains now are linguistic and cultural traces.

Certainly many Indian languages with relationships to Sanskrit (the ancient language of the Aryans) bear clear links with European languages, whilst some of the religious practices of the Aryans resemble those of the ancient Greeks. This does not mean that Sanskrit sprang from Greek or a European language, or that the European languages emerged from Sanskrit, but rather that all of these languages have evolved from an earlier language. We say that they belong to the Indo-European family of languages. Early texts, known as *Vedas*, were left by the Aryan civilization, which set down the correct way to behave in every aspect of life, be it religious, political, or cultural. Even now, the *Vedas* remain a foundation of Hinduism for millions of Indians.

DAWN OF HINDU EMPIRES

Throughout the centuries India's culture and history have been influenced by other peoples, and colonies of both the Greeks and Persians are referred to in the *Mahabharata* (an ancient Indian epic) in just the same way that other Indian peoples are. It is well known that Alexander the Great attempted the enormous task of conquering India around 2,500 years ago. He left colonies of Greeks in Bactria, an area around what is now Afghanistan, from which incursions into India occurred.

Would-be conquerors

This pattern was repeated by many different would-be conquerors over the millennia to come. While Alexander's attempted conquest of India (327–325 BC) was unsuccessful, and halted when the exhausted and demoralized Greek soldiers mutinied, their daring leader's impact on the Indian consciousness lasts until this day.

Even in the period of the Delhi Sultanates 1,000 years later, the Turkish emperor, Ala-ud-din, who ruled from AD 1296 to 1316, minted coins with an inscription describing himself as a second Alexander (Ala-ud-din Sikander Sani Khalji). His successor, Muhammad bin Tughluq, planned a mission to attack Afghanistan and battle through Alexander's route backwards to Iran. However, he had to cancel the plan in AD 1329, when it proved prohibitively expensive. The name Sikander remained popular amongst the Sultans, with another Sultan Ala-ud-din Sikander briefly occupying the throne from AD 1394–1395. The penultimate Delhi Sultan, Sikander Lodi who acceded to the throne in AD 1489 was actually an Afghan.

Expansion

Alexander was to provide immediate inspiration to the Mauryan emperor Chandragupta, who assumed power in the northwestern kingdom of Magadha (within the modern-day state of Bihar) in 322 BC, just one year after Alexander's death. While Chandragupta eventually renounced violence and became a Jain, his son Bindusara expanded the Mauryan empire, both to the east and the west.

However, the expansion was to reach its zenith under Chandragupta's grandson, Ashoka, who expanded the empire from Magadha to almost the whole of modern India and far into Afghanistan. Only the far south was spared and the extent of Ashoka's dominion was not to be surpassed until the British rule 2,000 years later. Legend tells us that Ashoka was finally horrified by the extent of the bloodshed that he had caused and embraced Buddhism, which was spread by his son and daughter as far as Sri Lanka and southeast Asia. Pillars and monuments with Buddhist inscriptions are in evidence in India, which date back from Ashoka's time and Buddhism dominated the sub-continent for a thousand years. Unfortunately, like Alexander before him, Ashoka left behind an inadequate imperial infrastructure and the empire collapsed soon after his death.

Land of empires

Until the arrival of the British, India was really a collection of smaller empires, states and principalities, rather than a true country. Noteworthy amongst the great dynastic empires that emerged was that of the Cholas, whose king, Rajaraja, conquered a wide territory stretching from Andhra Pradesh to southernmost Tamil Nadu 1,000 years ago. His monuments can still be seen, including the giant temples at Tanjore and Srirangam in southern India. Whether they were built to propitiate *karma*, reducing the debt of sin for thousands of deaths caused by conquest, or merely status symbols, these temples are a tribute to the architecture of the ancient Indians.

Another great city from the long period of Hindu power in southern India was Vijayanagar, now known as the white stone city of Hampi. Vijayanagar had a huge empire, like that of Tanjore in the time of greatest Chola power 500 years earlier. Vijayanagar finally fell into ruins after a period of political instability in the 16th century when four sultans from neighbouring empires, including Bijapur and Golconda (later to become Hyderabad) defeated the Hindu king, Rama Raja. The final conflict that ended the Hindu empire was the battle of Talikota in 1565 on the River Krishna, around 75 miles north of Vijayanagar.

MUSLIM CONQUEST OF INDIA

Muslim traders had sold horses and spices during the seventh century BC. After conquering Persia, Arabs occupied part of what is now Pakistan, but it was not until the eighth century that the weakness of the northern Hindu states allowed the first wave of Muslims from Afghanistan to penetrate into India. Gradually, as the ninth century continued, the northwest of the sub-continent was subject to incursions by an emerging Islamic empire. Power struggles within the Islamic empire meant that the centre of the caliphate in Iran would pass into the hands of Alptigin Samani, a governor of Turkic (Central Asian) descent. He established a Turkic dynasty in what is now Afghanistan. The Turkic ruler Sabuktigin Samani then defeated a coalition of Hindu forces and by the 11th century, his son Mahmoud adopted the title, Sultan. At this point Mahmoud crossed the River Indus and annexed the Punjab. Next, Sultan Mahmoud advanced to the river Ganges and crushed the important city of Mathura. He further progressed to Gujarat and captured the city of Somnath.

Mahmoud's successor Masoud, however, turned his attention to the east because of threats to eastern Iran. By the middle of the 12th century, Ghazni, the power base established by Mahmoud and Masoud in

Afghanistan was overthrown when its ruler, Sultan Bahram, was defeated by Emir Aladdin Hussein of Ghor in revenge for the killing of two princes from Ghor.

Later that century, Punjab and Sind were both seized by Shihabuddin Muhammad from Ghor. Indeed, by the end of the 12th century Muhammad Ghori had conquered Lahore and gained control over the whole Indus valley. However, when Muhammad Ghori's force of Turks, Afghans, Persians and Arabs advanced beyond the Punjab, it was defeated by a coalition of Hindu forces. Nevertheless, the next year, Ghori triumphed in a second battle with the Hindus, returning victorious to Afghanistan. His leading general, the Turk, Qutbuddin Aibak, went on to annexe Delhi and establish it as his headquarters. In the final years of the 12th century, Muhammad Ghori returned from Afghanistan to defeat the Hindu king of Varanasi (Benares).

The Delhi Sultanates

Another of Muhammad Ghori's generals, Ikhtiyaruddin Khilji conquered a large area of south Bihar and Bengal. The conquests continued, and in 1206 Muhammad Ghori was assassinated. The Turkish general Qutbuddin Aibak, once a slave, inherited a large sultanate in northern India, but then shifted the capital from Delhi to Lahore for the rest of his lifetime.

For the next 300 years the so-called Delhi Sultanates were the dominant force in northern India. In the first century of their power the sultans struggled with Mongol attacks from the northwest of the subcontinent, as well as resistance from the Hindus. Very gradually a degree of fusion between Hindu and Muslim cultures became possible, and this is visible in areas ranging from architecture to cuisine.

Qutbuddin Aibak's son-in-law, Iltimush, proclaimed himself 'the Great Sultan'. He wore a robe of honour conferred on him by the Caliph of Baghdad, a city that was then the centre of the Islamic world. Unlike Aibak, Iltimush, who was a learned man, proved to be a great patron of the arts and his monuments are still visible in Delhi today.

8

At the same time, the Mongol forces of Genghis Khan established control over a massive area including regions of China, Turkey and Afghanistan. Genghis even went as far as to cross the River Indus in pursuit of a rebellious prince and it was only Iltimush's cooperation with Genghis in denying asylum to the fugitive, that prevented a Mongol invasion of India.

The rise of the Mongol Empire

After his death, the empire of Iltimush started to fragment until Sultan Iltimush's daughter Raziyya was able to seize power. Raziyya was opposed by Turkic forces who supported her incompetent brother, Muizuddin Bahram, and finally she was killed by Hindu rebels. After the death of Genghis Khan, the weakness of the remnants of Iltimush's empire made it easy for the Mongols to sack Lahore. However, when Genghis' grandson, Hulagu reached into Punjab he was repelled by the Muslim forces in India. The Mongols went on to overthrow the power centre of the Islamic empire, Baghdad itself. In 1259 their leader, Mongke, died and the Mongol empire, which might have threatened India, was split into four.

The Indian sultan, Nasiruddin Mahmoud entered into diplomatic relations with the ambassador of Hulagu, who ruled the quadrant of the Mongol empire to the northwest of India. Despite Nasiruddin Mahmoud's strengthening of the Muslim empire, with the death of the Mongol Hulagu, Mongol forces sporadically raided the subcontinent. When a ruthless new leader, Balban emerged amongst India's Muslims, an efficient intelligence service was set up. A revolt against the Delhi Sultanate by Tughril Khan, the governor of Bengal, was crushed. Unfortunately, Balban's son was killed by Mongols on the northwest frontier. Balban's grandson was assassinated and the 70-year-old, Jalaluddin Feroz Shah from the northwest of Pakistan, seized the throne in Delhi allowing thousands of Mongols to settle near Delhi, as long as they converted to Islam.

Aladdin to Timur

The next major figure amongst the Turkish Muslims was Aladdin who, in the early 14th century, strengthened the empire and prevented rebellions by strictly controlling the imperial purse-strings. Aladdin declared himself a second Alexander (Sikander). After his death a series of power struggles ensued, which only ended after the ruthless Muhammad Adil Bin Tughluq murdered his father, the Sultan, by causing an elephant stampede. While he was a great intellectual, a patron of the arts and a poet, Tughluq was known for dreadful cruelty, not only on a personal level, but also in crushing rebel forces. Nevertheless, even Tughluq had to resort to bribery to hold back Mongol forces from the imperial frontier.

However, halfway through the 14th century Tughluq fell ill and died in pursuit of a Gujurati rebel leader. Without a direct successor, his cousin Feroz Shah II Tughluq, a more compassionate man, took over the empire and banned torture as a form of punishment. The Sultan had mixed success against his enemies, achieving victory against the king of Orissa and destroying the temple at Puri, but handing the province back in return for an annual tribute. He also failed to take control of Bengal, which remained independent for 200 years. Feroz Shah II brought two Ashokan pillars from what is now known as the Punjab and Uttar Pradesh to Delhi, one of which is still a tourist attraction at Ferozabad.

After the death of Feroz Shah II there was a rapid succession of weak rulers. While the divided Turkish Muslims of northern India were fighting each other, the forces of the neighbouring Mongol empire, led by the ruler of Uzbekistan, Timur the Great, crossed the Indus. Timur's advance proved unstoppable and after executing 100,000 Hindu prisoners, Timur conquered Delhi and continued the slaughter. However, within just a few years Timur died in Uzbekistan and the throne passed to his son, Shah Rukh.

Afghan dynasty

While a Turkish region was still present in northern India, the division of power during the first half of the 15th century allowed the former governor of the Punjab, Bahlul Lodi, who was of Afghan descent, to seize power and begin a short-lived Afghan dynasty. Bahlul was succeeded by his son, Sikander Lodi, who established a new capital at Agra.

Meanwhile, trouble was brewing in Uzbekistan once more, when Babur, the boy king, inherited the throne of the Uzbek region called Fergana. Babur was a descendant of both Timur on his father's side and Genghis Khan on his mother's side. In the year 1500, Babur consolidated his power in Uzbekistan by conquering Samarkand, his ancestor Timur's seat of power.

The end of the Delhi Sultanates

At the same time, Portugal began forcefully to establish a small trading colony in the southern region of India, which is now Kerala. Another southern king, Krishna Deva Raya II had expanded a huge empire centred at the city of Vijayanagar (now known as the stone city of Hampi in northern Karnataka).

Sikander Lodi's son, Ibrahim proved to be a somewhat irresponsible ruler, antagonizing the nobles. At the same time the Mongol, Babur, made aggressive incursions into the Punjab, then based himself at Kabul. Finally, one of Ibrahim Lodi's relatives, Daulat Khan, invited Babur to topple Ibrahim. Three years later, in 1526, with more encouragement from Ibrahim's family, Babur confronted Ibrahim Lodi at the Battle of Panipat. Ibrahim was killed and the battle was won decisively by the Mongols (referred to as Mughals in India), who then ruled most of India for nearly 300 years.

THE MUGHAL ERA

The Mughals had an inestimable effect on India, shaping our perception of the country with tremendous achievements in art, cuisine, dance, language and architecture. They also spread their control of India deeper into the south than any dynasty since Ashoka's.

The rule of Akbar

However, the future of the empire was uncertain under its first rulers, Babur and his son Humayun. In fact, during his reign, Humayun temporarily lost control of the empire to an Afghan leader. Fortunately for the dynasty, his eldest son, Akbar, became a wise and powerful ruler who expanded the empire. He also proclaimed a different religious point of view, namely that Hindus, Muslims and Sikhs were all worshipping the same God and that the distinctions between the faiths were artificial. At first he based his capital at Agra, where he constructed the impressive Red Fort, which is still standing today. However, he decided that a new, impressive capital, Fatehpur Sikri (the City of Victory at Sikri) should be built some distance from Agra. Even now the enormous arch and walls of his fortified city are breathtaking. Akbar later shifted his capital to Lahore, in present-day Pakistan, before moving back to Agra on the River Jamuna as Fatehpur Sikri was short of water. Akbar was a Mughal born in India, and he cared deeply about his subjects. He even showed compassion to his son, Salim (later to be known as Jahangir) when Salim staged a rebellion and declared himself emperor. This was a remarkable act of mercy from Akbar by the standards of the times.

Jahangir

Jahangir, whose rule started in 1605, was a man of varied interests who tried to treat all his subjects fairly. But like many of the Mughals, he was something of an alcoholic and also an opium addict. He also committed many acts of cruelty, like having his eldest son's eyes stitched shut after he staged a rebellion. He had seemingly forgotten or disregarded that his father, Akbar, had shown mercy to Jahangir when he had staged his own rebellion.

Shah Jahan

However, it was Jahangir's third son who, through sheer ruthlessness was to be the next to seize power. He did this by murdering his two older brothers and when Jahangir died, blinded and then killed his younger brother Shahriyar, who had made a bid for power and declared himself emperor. When the remaining princes who had a claim to power were dead and the throne was safely in Shah Jahan's grasp, he became one of the most respected of the Mughal emperors.

Shah Jahan is most fondly remembered today for his architectural legacy, especially the Taj Mahal, a mausoleum for his second and favourite wife, Mumtaz Mahal.

History was to repeat itself and as his sons increased in power, another power struggle ensued. While Shah Jahan favoured his moderate first son, Dara Shikoh who believed in religious harmony between Hindus and Muslims, it was his third son, Aurangzeb who emerged victorious.

Aurangzeb

After claiming the throne and imprisoning his father in the Red Fort at Agra, within sight of the Taj Mahal, Aurangzeb finally captured his eldest brother, Dara, and had him beheaded. Aurangzeb was also instrumental in the indictment and execution of his younger brother, Murad Baksh, who had been an ally in the War of Succession, but later turned against him. Aurangzeb was something of a religious zealot, and this meant that he deplored alcoholism and instituted customs duties and taxes, which only non-Muslims were liable to pay. He also had the ninth Sikh guru killed; a move which drove the Sikhs to militancy.

Aurangzeb's sons rebelled against his command, but the Emperor proved capable of maintaining control. He defeated the British East India Company, capturing Bombay, but then allowed the British to go back to business as usual after they had paid large war indemnities. Aurangzeb stretched the empire to its farthest reaches at Tanjore, deep in the south of India.

BRITISH RAJ – THE JEWEL IN THE CROWN

The final period of the Mughal Empire, the 18th century, is notable as a time of imperial weakness. The lack of an effective navy, combined with an outmoded and indolent army, led to a gradual fragmentation of India into smaller states. An invasion of forces led by Nadir Shah, an Afghan ruler from Persia in 1739, dealt a devastating blow to the Mughals. Delhi was looted and the Kohinoor diamond, the Peacock Throne and many other treasures were taken. The empire broke into smaller states ruled by Nawabs, in regions such as Oudh, Bengal, and the Deccan, while the French, British and Portuguese strengthened their hold on the trading territories that they occupied. Britain emerged as the dominant power, and Robert Clive re-took the previously British territory of Calcutta in Bengal, from Siraj al Dawla after the Battle of Plassey in 1757.

British dominance in India

Another victory cementing British dominance in India was the victory of Major Hector Munro at the Battle of Baksar in 1764. Here, the army of the East India Company defeated an alliance of Mughal forces with the Muslim leaders of Bengal and Oudh. In this battle, in which the Indian coalition attempted to re-take Patna from the East India Company, the British force of 7,500 defeated a coalition four times as large. Robert Clive then became the governor of a large region of northeast India known as the Bengal Presidency and restored the Mughal emperor, Shah Alam II, who opposed the British in the Battle of Baksar. However, the East India Company had extensive trading rights and were willing to pay a substantial annual fee to their puppet ruler.

The East India Company

In the latter part of the 18th century, the development of cotton mills and machine-loomed textiles in Britain severely hit the revenue of the East India Company, which depended to a large extent on the sale of its hand-loomed Indian cotton. After the suicide of Robert Clive, the new governor of Bengal, Warren Hastings, hired out his army to the neighbouring region of Oudh to defend it from invasion. The East India Company increasingly demonstrated that it was becoming a political entity, as well as a financial concern.

Another victory for the British, against the Marathas on the west coast of India in 1775 added to the power of the Company, while the American War of Independence in 1776 created a market for Indian-grown cotton when American cotton was denied to Britain.

In the latter part of the 1780s with Earl Cornwallis as Governor, laws were passed by the Company which ensured that higher posts in the military and the judiciary only went to the British and not to Indians. An attack by Tipu Sultan, 'the Tiger of Mysore', against the British protectorate of Travancore in the south of India was quashed by Lord Cornwallis in 1789, and British power in the south was extended to the southwestern Malabar coast. Within the next few years, the East India Company grabbed a succession of territories, again defeating the Marathas and extending to the southernmost parts of the subcontinent. Opium also proved to be an invaluable Indian product that the British could trade with China.

While puppet rulers were maintained from 1807 until 1947, India replaced the lost colony of America as the 'jewel in the crown' of the British Empire. However, just like in the Americas, unfair treatment of colonial subjects by the British led to wars of independence. The British achieved what no other conquerors had before, control of the entire subcontinent. While they undoubtedly have had a lasting influence on Indian culture, introducing tea-drinking, cricket, railway and postal networks, the British are remembered for a high-handed attitude to their Indian subjects. Also, unlike the Mughals, the British had not really settled in India to become in some way naturalized, but rather were using the subcontinent as a source of revenue for Britain.

Rebellion

Even in the early 19th century, trouble began. A localized mutiny occurred at Barrackpore in 1824 and again in 1852, when Bengali soldiers objected to being sent to Burma where differences in caste would no longer apply. Things finally came to a head in 1857, when a new rifle, the Enfield was introduced. Indian soldiers were required by their British officers to bite open the end of the cartridge before loading the gun. Because the jackets of the cartridges were greased with animal fat from both cows and pigs, Hindus and Muslims alike were revolted. This, combined with a general concern that the British intended to force them to become Christians, set off a rebellion in northern India. Thousands of Bengali soldiers marched to Delhi to enlist the support of the puppet emperor, Bahadur Shah in their uprising. The 40,000 rebels were defeated by the British near Delhi and whilst most of the Indian garrisons were in revolt, the thrust of the rebellion shifted to the cities of Lucknow, Jhansi and Kanpur.

At Kanpur 3,000 rebels forced a British garrison to surrender, but then massacred their prisoners in reprisal for an execution of mutineers by the British. Ultimately, all territories occupied by the rebels were recaptured in just 13 months and the British were back in control.

While the American War of Independence disrupted the supply of cotton to Britain in the 18th century, the same thing happened when the American Civil War broke out in 1861, but this time India was ready to step into the breach and the British cotton plantations in India profited greatly from the situation.

Lord Curzon

As the 19th century drew to a close, efforts were made to set up an Indian government in which Indian people participated. But in reality the Indians were still only allowed to discuss serious issues, such as the budget, and not make decisions. The Viceroy, Lord Curzon, made a number of decisions which had repercussions for India's future. On the positive side, Curzon established the Archaeological Society of India to preserve the ancient buildings of the subcontinent, and set up a department to increase areas that were irrigated.

However, he also expanded the borders of the state of Jammu and Kashmir into what was Chinese territory, giving rise to a border that is still disputed today. In addition, the Bengal Presidency, already a hotbed of political unrest, was further upset in 1905. Lord Curzon partitioned the state into mainly Muslim Eastern Bengal and Assam (with its capital in Dacca, now the capital of Bangladesh) and mainly Hindu Western Bengal, whose capital was Calcutta (now known as Kolkata, still the chief city of present-day Bengal). The partition lasted until 1911 and was extremely unpopular. During this period, bomb attacks were staged by revolutionaries against British officials and the Indian Congress party urged the boycotting of British goods, which were publicly burnt in protest. At the same time the British took steps to give Muslims superior political rights. Even today, many Indians associate the British with a 'divide and rule' policy.

Into the twentieth century

During the early part of the 20th century (from 1911–1925), the British made their own contribution to Indian architecture in the form of New Delhi. In fact, the British city was the eighth in a succession of 'Delhis', which followed those of the Delhi Sultanate and Shah Jahan of the Mughals. While the names of the impressive buildings left by the architect Sir Edwin Lutyens have been changed, they are still in use and the British War Memorial Arch has become the India Gate. What was the British Viceroy Palace is now the President's Mansion, better known as Rashtrapati Bhavan. Even the present-day Indian Parliament is situated in what was the British Imperial Legislative Council.

INDIAN INDEPENDENCE MOVEMENT

In spite of the hardships suffered by Indians, when the British Empire was confronted with the First World War, India answered the call and two million Indians left their country to support Britain in its war effort. During the First World War, the veteran political campaigner, Mohandas Karamchand Gandhi (later to be known as Mahatma [meaning 'Great Spirit'] Gandhi) came to India from South Africa. Jinnah, the leader of the Muslim League, a group that had been favoured by the British, joined forces with the Congress Party to demand the right of self-rule for India in recognition of India's war effort. The British majority defeated the Indians, who were under-represented in the Indian Legislative Council (not yet a true parliament) and tough legislation was enacted which allowed detention without trial for any suspected Indian 'terrorist'.

During this heavy-handed time, Brigadier General Dyer ordered the machine-gunning of hundreds of unarmed civilian protesters at a protest in Amritsar. In response, Gandhi called for civil disobedience. Between the First and Second World Wars a British Labour government tried to placate the campaigners by offering India the same status as Canada and Australia, but for India nothing less than independence was acceptable.

After the Great Depression of the 1930s and then the Second World War, Britain was severely weakened and was in the twilight days of its empire. While Gandhi's movement relied on non-violent strike action and peaceful methods, others, such as Jinnah were more aggressive vocally, or even militarily. One such was Subash Chandra Bose, who collaborated with both the Germans and the Japanese during the Second World War and recruited an army (albeit ineffectual) against the British.

Independence

In the end the result was inevitable and Lord Mountbatten was called in to oversee the independence of India in 1947. However, by this stage – with longstanding independence campaigns by Jinnah's Muslim League, which demanded a separate Muslim state, as well as by Congress and other groups, which were predominantly Hindu – massive rioting occurred, with Hindus and Sikhs involved in horribly violent clashes with Muslims. There was no choice but to partition the country into India and Pakistan, the latter being a predominantly Muslim state.

However, the partition was rushed and while Muslims crossed from India to Pakistan and Hindus and Sikhs from Pakistan crossed to India, enormous numbers of people were massacred in communal violence. The partition was not the last word on the violence. The region of Jammu and Kashmir, a predominantly Muslim state with a Hindu ruler who preferred to maintain a degree of autonomy, belatedly decided to stay with India when Pakistani forces pouring into Kashmir approached the state capital, Srinagar. The situation was complicated by the fact that Jammu was mainly Hindu, while Kashmir was predominantly Muslim, but no-one was prepared to further divide the state. War raged over Kashmir from the birth of India in 1947 until 1949 when India gained overall control.

INDIA 1947 TO THE PRESENT DAY

'We had made a tryst with destiny and now the time has come to redeem our pledge', so said Nehru on the eve of Indian independence on 15th August 1947. While independence was cause for all Indians to rejoice, the accompanying partition of India was no matter to celebrate. A new country called Pakistan was created with two flanks separated by Indian territory. Many Muslims and Hindus found themselves living as threatened minorities in the highly-charged atmosphere of newly-independent Pakistan or India. Massive population exchange ensued. Nearly 14.5 million people crossed the border and half a million people perished. Mahatma Gandhi himself fell to an assassin's bullet less than a year after independence.

Jawaharlal Nehru

Jawaharlal Nehru became India's first prime minister and his Congress party continued to capture most seats across the country for the rest of his lifetime. He built large dams and steel mills, and introduced five-year plans to boost the Indian economy. He refused to kowtow to either of the super-powers and maintained Indian independence in foreign affairs. But relationships with both China and Pakistan were frosty, and a war with China in 1962 dealt a blow to his prestige, both nationally and internationally. After a gap of two years following his death in 1964, his daughter, Indira Gandhi (no relation to Mahatma Gandhi) assumed the post of prime minister.

Indira Gandhi

Initially underestimated, Indira Gandhi turned out to be an astute politician, eliminating her rivals and power-brokers who tried to control her. Her rule was marked by a war with Pakistan that resulted in the creation of Bangladesh, greater socialism and nationalization of domestic industries, and cold relations with the USA. She imposed a state of emergency on the country which made her unpopular and led to her losing an election in 1977. The non-Congress government that followed squabbled endlessly and Indira Gandhi returned to power again in 1980. Her second stint was marked by disturbances in the states of the Punjab and Assam. Her supposedly high-handed techniques in handling disturbances in the Punjab alienated the Sikh community, and she was killed by her own Sikh bodyguards in 1984. Her son Rajiv Gandhi returned to power with a large majority of seats in 1985. Known initially as Mr Clean, he embarked on a series of economic reforms that continue to this day. However the Congress party's monopoly over power in India had ended. New regional, sectarian and caste-based parties had emerged. He lost the elections in 1989 and was killed by a suicide bomber of the Sri Lankan Tamil Tigers.

After the Congress Party monopoly

In the two decades after Rajiv Gandhi's death, a variety of parties including the Congress party have ruled the country, often with slim parliamentary majorities. Continuing government with different political parties has shown the vibrancy of Indian democracy. Continued economic liberalization has been the hallmark of most of the recent Indian governments. India, never a signatory of Nuclear Non-proliferation Treaty, detonated a series of nuclear bombs in 1998 making it a nuclear power.

All through its history, independent India has had a turbulent history with Pakistan, having fought four wars and coming dangerously close to fighting again a few years ago. Since both countries are nuclear powers now, their stand-off receives world attention.

2
General Information

GEOGRAPHICAL DIVISIONS

India is a huge country – the seventh largest in the world – and in many respects it is more helpful to think of the sub-continent as resembling continental Europe, rather than a single country, such as France or Germany.

Geographically it borders Pakistan on the west; China, Nepal, and Bhutan on the north-east; and Bangladesh and Myanmar on the east. In the south are the island nations of Sri Lanka and Maldives.

In the northwest in Pakistan, the Kirthar and also the Sulaiman mountain ranges provide a physical barrier to the subcontinent. Similarly, where the northern most regions of Pakistan and India (now the disputed region of Jammu and Kashmir) overlap the north eastern region of Afghanistan, the Hindu Kush (meaning, 'Hindu Killer') mountains provide another barrier. Where Jammu and Kashmir overlap with China, the Karakoram range provides something of a barrier, which again includes a small disputed border between India and China. Moving east across the mountains of the north, one encounters the Himalayas, where India borders on the mountainous country of Nepal. In the northeast the mountains continue along the borders of Tibet and Bhutan. South of the mountains a tributary of the River Ganges joins with the River Brahmaputra and then empties into the Bay of Bengal in the land of a thousand rivers, Bangladesh.

If we cross through the narrow region of India between Nepal, Tibet, Bhutan and Bangladesh, we reach the most northeastern part of India. This remote pocket of land, the so-called North-Eastern Territories (Assam, Arunachal Pradesh, Nagaland, Meghalaya, Manipur, Mizoram and Tripura), is spanned by most of the River Brahmaputra. The boundaries of the North-Eastern Territories are provided by the mountainous regions of Tibet and Bhutan in the north, Bangladesh in the south-west, and the hilly jungles of Myanmar (formerly Burma) in the south-east. The remaining borders of India are simply provided by the Arabian Sea in the west and in the east, the Bay of Bengal which joins onto the subcontinent from the Indian Ocean.

Historically (and prehistorically), the most important barriers are the mountains of Pakistan and Afghanistan. This is because they are only passable via narrow crossings at the Bolan Pass and Ghomal Pass (through Pakistan) and via the Khyber Pass through Afghanistan. Invaders, including Alexander the Great, the Turkic Sultans and the Mughals, amongst many others, chose these routes to enter what is now known as India. It was only when naval powers, such as the Dutch, Portuguese and British turned their attention to India that her sea borders became vulnerable.

The River Indus in Pakistan, with its five branches in the Punjab (meaning 'five rivers'), has also proved an obstacle to many invaders. The year after Alexander crossed the Hindu Kush mountains, he had to cross the Indus to fight the battle of Hydapses against King Porus. Porus was the leader of the region between the two branches of the Indus, known to the Greeks as Hydapses and Akensines (but more familiar to Punjabis as Jhelum and Chenab). While the battle was a resounding victory for Alexander, he was impressed by the dignity of Porus and the two became allies. Three more rivers of the Punjab remained as barriers, and by the time Alexander had fought his way to the last river (the River Bias, which is today known as the Sutlej), his exhausted and demoralized men were in revolt. Finally, Alexander decided to travel down the Indus by boat, having been outfaced by the sheer magnitude of the task of conquering India.

Even within India certain looser geographic boundaries exist, such as the Western Ghats. This range of mountains runs parallel to the west coast from the states of Maharashtra to Kerala, with the scenic Malabar Coast nestling between the mountains and the sea.

Rivers also act as natural borders within India, like the River Tapti which marks the northern border of the state of Maharashtra, and the River Wardha at the eastern border of the same state.

The many rivers that criss-cross India are no longer significant as geographic boundaries, although they are still a source of political division. The Kaveri river in southern India provides a good example when the construction of a dam in the state of Karnataka blocked the flow of water into the neighbouring state of Tamil Nadu. This recently caused a political row and outraged Tamil farmers.

THE POLITICAL SYSTEM

India is the largest democracy in the world and with the exception of Mrs Gandhi's controversial two-year emergency seizure of power in 1975 has maintained a democratic system since its Constitution was adopted in 1950. Other South Asian countries (notably Pakistan, Bangladesh and Myanmar [Burma]) have failed to maintain democracy.

India's main parties are Congress (which has fragmented since its original political dominance) and BJP, Bharatiya Janata Party, or Indian People's Party. India has a President, who is elected for five years by an electoral college like the USA, on a 'first-past-the-post' system like the British. In common with the UK, the Prime Minister is the head of central government. Minor parties are far more significant than in the UK or US, and are sometimes associated with particular states or regions. West Bengal and Kerala are dominated by Communist, while Tamil Nadu has a strong political identity, as has Punjab. These are just a few of the many parties, which is perhaps to be expected in a country with so many different creeds, states, castes and affiliations. While the country is holding together as a secular democracy, the North-Eastern Territories have secessionist elements who resort to terrorism, and the dispute between India and Pakistan over Jammu and Kashmir has led to four wars and an ongoing terrorism problem. Furthermore a Naxalite (Maoist) movement which resorts to terrorism to resist central government, has spread across wide stretches of rural India.

On a cultural level, Indians express pride in their country and seem to give their politicians the benefit of the doubt, in spite of widespread corruption at every level. India has a healthy freedom of the press and satirical cartoons often appear, lampooning regional politicians who manipulate politics at a state level in a laughable way. While not as unscrupulous and aggressive as the British press, Indian journalists bravely expose corruption (sometimes at the cost of their lives). By reading a variety of Indian newspapers (each of which has its own political bias) you will soon gain an appreciation of the most notable figures in contemporary Indian politics.

Political divisions

On a regional level, India is divided into 28 states and seven union territories. All the states and union territory of Delhi and Puducherry have regional elected governments. The other five union territories are under the president's rule and have administrators appointed. Further states and union territories are divided into smaller units called districts. There are about 600 districts in India.

State territories of India	
1. Andhra Pradesh	15. Maharashtra
2. Arunachal Pradesh	16. Manipur
3. Assam	17. Meghalaya
4. Bihar	18. Mizoram
5. Chhattisgarh	19. Nagaland
6. Goa	20. Orissa
7. Gujarat	21. Punjab
8. Haryana	22. Rajasthan
9. Himachal Pradesh	23. Sikkim
10. Jammu and Kashmir	24. Tamil Nadu
11. Jharkhand	25. Tripura
12. Karnataka	26. Uttar Pradesh
13. Kerala	27. Uttarakhand
14. Madhya Pradesh	28. West Bengal

Union territories of India	
1. Andaman and Nicobar Islands	5. Lakshadweep
2. Chandigarh	6. National Capital Territory of Delhi
3. Dadra and Nagar Haveli	7. Puducherry
4. Daman and Diu	

RELIGION IN INDIA

In the mind of the foreign visitor, religion certainly provides some of the most iconographic images of life in India. Whether we think of minarets, temples, stupas (monuments) or saffron-robed priests deep in meditation, we expect to encounter religion in India. All of these well-established images will be found in India and the visitor will not be disappointed, but there is far more to see than this and your Indian friends will be only too happy to answer the questions of an open-minded foreigner.

Religion is an important part of life in every region of the subcontinent. While Hinduism (a very broad and ambiguous term in itself) is the major faith (about 81% of Indians are Hindus), there are also many Muslims (about 13% of the population, and often there may be a Muslim part of town). Sikhs make up about two per cent of the population and, perhaps surprisingly, there are quite a lot of Christians, and some Jains and Buddhists. Small communities of Jews and Zoroastrians (Parsees) are also localized to particular regions, but in most cases you are unlikely to encounter these groups.

While Hindus can be found all over India, other religions are sometimes irregularly dispersed over the subcontinent. The majority of Sikhs are found in the state of Punjab, and a large number of 'Syrian' Christians in the southern state of Kerala which contains roughly one third each of Hindus, Muslims and Christians. There are large communities of Jains in north Karnataka, Gujarat and Rajsathan. Large cosmopolitan cities may often have representatives of each community, sometimes with preferred professions, such as Jains who are often involved in non-violent businesses or professions.

Christianity

Christianity has a long history in India, and although never a dominant religion it has, like Buddhism, provided an attractive alternative for low-caste Hindus who have wanted to seek a better life through religious conversion. Christians are relatively more numerous in regions that traditionally have had longstanding trading and colonial contacts with Europe. Goa, which was a Portuguese colony from Mughal times until 1961 has a strong Christian community, as has the nearby area of Konkan in north Karnataka. Kerala's Christian cultural influence has been so strong that (even though it is only one third Christian) beef is even eaten by some Hindus there. Large churches and cathedrals can be found in cities such as Bangalore and Mysore, and in Tamil Nadu there is even a place called Nazareth, which is staunchly Christian. The strength of the church in southern India is not necessarily a result of Portuguese missionaries, but rather is explained by a visit to Kerala by Thomas the apostle in AD 52, where he set up a number of so-called 'Syrian' churches. Thomas went on to travel to the east coast of India and preached at Mylapore in what is now Chennai. Although Thomas met with stiff opposition on the east coast and was martyred by King Misdeos of Mylapore, the saint left his legacy in the form of a Christian community in Chennai.

Jains and Buddhists

The Jains are quite similar to Buddhists and place non-violence as the highest virtue, and while both Jains and Buddhists are vegetarian, Jains are not even permitted to eat root vegetables because of the violence involved in their harvesting. And while Buddha never intended to be worshipped, he frequently will be. It can be said that Jains do not worship God, but rather the 'supersoul', which is a fascinating point of discussion.

Islam

Islam in India is the second-most practised religion after Hinduism. Muslims worship one God, Allah, and strictly avoid eating pork. Often they will avoid contact with dogs, because it is undesirable for a Muslim to touch any wet parts of a dog. This is probably good advice all round in India as rabies is a serious problem and the slightest scratch from a dog (or cat, or monkey) or drop of saliva in a wound can prove fatal. Muslims in India have a reputation for cooking delicious spicy food, a fact that the authors can attest to!

Hinduism

Hinduism, although superficially simple, is the most complex religion to explain. It consists of a great many religious and philosophical viewpoints and opinions, which in fact is possibly its greatest strength. While it is often said that Hindus recognize three gods; Brahma (the creator), Vishnu (the preserver) and Shiva (the destroyer), all of which are necessary to the cosmic balance, it is also said that they worship one God (just as many Christians regard God the Father, Jesus Christ the Son, and the Holy Spirit as three aspects of one God). You will soon come to appreciate that Hindus worship many gods (such as the elephant-headed Ganesh the remover of obstacles, Agni the fire god and Surya the sun god) and goddesses (such as Saraswathi the goddess of learning and the arts, Kali the goddess of destruction and Durga the warrior goddess who triumphed over the buffalo demon). These gods and goddesses are often inter-related. They cannot simply be described as the god of one thing, such as 'fire' or 'rain', but they have characteristics and personalities that stem from many legends and stories which may even contradict each other. It is generally accepted that each of these gods and goddesses manifest some aspect of the divine in a way that is easily comprehensible to the layman.

Vishnu and Shiva are perhaps the most popular gods although Vishnu is reputed to have manifested himself on Earth as at least ten different avatars or forms. Of these Rama and Krishna are the most frequently worshipped, but Vishnu may alternatively be represented as Sri Venkateshwara (a resplendent bridegroom) worshipped at the nationally famous temple at Tirupathi in Andhra Pradesh. While lots of Hindus accept Vishnu and Shiva as two sides of the same coin, Vaishnavites and Shaivites worship one form. In fact some Vaishnavites may go so far as to regard Shiva as a demon.

Even within the followers of Vishnu, there are a great many sects, in much the same way that Christianity has Catholics and Protestants, and Protestants may be Methodist, Baptist, Lutheran, etc. Sects often follow a Swami, or holy man, who may be a living reincarnation of an earlier saint (followers of Swaminaryan, and also of Sai Baba) or dead (followers of Swami Prabhupada, the holy teacher of ISKCON [the International Society for Krishna Consciousness], familiar as 'Hare Krishnas' in the west, for their popular mantra). These saints may actually be regarded as incarnations of God, like Swaminaryan, who is believed to be an earthly incarnation of Vishnu and is popular amongst many Gujaratis. Similarly, Sai Baba is regarded as the summation of Vishnu, Shiva and all other gods into the form of one man and is worshipped all over India. Different states emphasize different gods. One of Shiva's sons, Murrugan, is only worshipped in southern India, while the other, Ganesh is worshipped all over the country (especially in Karnataka and particularly in Gujarat and Maharashtra). The goddesses, Durga and Kali are very popular in West Bengal, while in Tamil Nadu they may be substituted by the ancient goddess of the village, and the home, Mariamman. In fact there are Hindu Tamils who worship Mary, the mother of Jesus as a kind of goddess, too.

Hindu gods

The flexibility of Hinduism accepts new forms of God and they are worshipped by all Hindus regardless of schools of beliefs.

The major gods
They form the core of Hindu belief.
Brahma: the Creator
Vishnu: the Protector
Shiva: the Destroyer
Goddess Lakshmi: Vishnu's wife and Goddess of Wealth
Goddess Parvathi: Shiva's Consort and Goddess of Strength
Goddess Saraswathi: the Goddess of Knowledge

The Vedic gods
These deities are listed in the ancient Vedic texts and are similar to Greek and Roman mythological gods.
Indra: Chief of Vedic Gods
Surya: the Sun God
Agni: the Fire God
Vayu: the God of Air

Varuna: the God of Rains
Yama: the God of Death
Kubera: the God of Wealth
Chandra: the Moon God
Prithvi: the God of Earth
Naga: the Snake God

Forms of God Vishnu

The following are the various avatars (forms) Lord Vishnu is said to have taken to rescue his followers from evil.
Matsyavatara: Vishnu as a fish
Kurmavatara: Vishnu as a tortoise
Varahavatar: Vishnu as a boar
Narasimhavatara: the half-lion, half-man
Vamanavatara: the dwarf
Parasurama: Rama with an axe
Rama: the prince of Ayodhya
Balarama: brother of Krishna
Krishna: the prince of Mathura
Buddha: the enlightened one
Kalki: the final incarnation (yet to come)

Wives, sons, relatives and friends

Ganesh: the elephant headed God and the remover of obstacles. Son of Shiva and Parvathi. Ganesh is the favourite God for the majority of Hindus.
Kartikeyan: son of Shiva and Parvathi. Also known as Murugan and Subramanya.
Hanuman: son of Vayu and a source of spiritual strength to bachelors.
Sita: wife of Rama
Lakshman: brother of Rama

Sikhism

The newest major religion, Sikhism, was founded in 1469 by Guru Nanak, who was born in what is now Pakistan as a Hindu. He later became a Sufi Muslim, before studying many religions and deciding that too many barriers were placed between mankind and oneness with God. Guru Nanak came up with the solution of Sikhism which is followed by 20 million Indians, mostly in Punjab, and can be regarded as a synthesis of positive aspects of both Islam and Hinduism. In common with Islam, idol-worship is forbidden as are any distinctions on the basis of caste. There was a total of ten Sikh teachers, or Gurus, starting with Nanak and ending when Gobind Singh died in 1708, each of whom contributed to their holy book (the Adi Granth – original book) which is itself regarded as a final Guru.

LANGUAGES

When educated foreigners are asked which language the Indians speak, they will often confidently tell you that it is Hindi. In fact, over 1,000 dialects are spoken in the subcontinent, with 22 major regional languages recognized. It is certainly true that Hindi is the official and most widely-spoken language in India and it will prove a valuable asset if you live in the north of India to learn a little of this. In fact, Hindi is either spoken or understood from Pakistan, Jammu and Kashmir in the west and north to Bihar and West Bengal in the east, and even as far south as Maharashtra and the major city of Andhra Pradesh, Hyderabad, which is a thriving centre for new biotech businesses.

Another language that is spoken amongst the Muslims in India is Urdu. Although Hindi and Urdu sound largely similar, there is a greater use of Sanskrit-derived words and script in Hindi, with more Arabic-derived words and script in Urdu and a lot of overlap between the two. While most of the states in northern India have their own regional languages, such as Punjabi, Gujarati and Bengali, there is some relationship between these languages and Hindi, in the way that Italian resembles Spanish or French. The popularity of Hindi movies in the north means that the Hindi language will prove helpful over vast swathes of the country. However, to the English-speaking foreigner the popularity of Hindi in the north is a double-edged sword, for while the company offering you a job in the subcontinent may assure you that English is spoken in India, the English language is less likely to be understood outside the working environment in northern India. Quite reasonably the onus is on the foreigner to make a little effort to learn this language, so beloved of Bollywood.

The situation is rather different in the southern Indian states of Karnataka, Tamil Nadu, Kerala and wide stretches of Andhra Pradesh. Although the region of India in which Hindi is not widely spoken is comparatively small, it contains a number of commercially important cities, such as Bangalore (Bengaluru) in Karnataka, Chennai (Madras) in Tamil Nadu, Trivandrum (Tiruvananthapuram) in Kerala, and Hyderabad in Andhra Pradesh (although Urdu is useful in Hyderabad). Moreover, when some of these cities reach saturation (notably Bangalore), business is anticipated to shift to nearby centres such as Mysore (a historical city three or four hours away from Bangalore by road or rail). Each of these southern states has its own language, with Malayalam, the language of Kerala resembling the Tamil language of Tamil Nadu. Telugu, the language spoken in Andhra Pradesh is the second most widely-spoken in India and has some relationship to both Kannada, which is spoken in Karnataka, and Tamil. Without the statewide acceptance of Hindi in this southern region, English is much more popular and so an English-speaking foreigner can manage without too much difficulty, bearing in mind that Indian English has its own unique characteristics (see Chapter 3).

Indian languages	
Language	Region spoken
Assamese	Assam
Bengali	Andaman and Nicobar Islands, Tripura, West Bengal
Bodo	Assam
Dogri	Jammu and Kashmir
Gujarati	Dadra and Nagar Haveli, Daman and Diu, Gujarat

Hindi	Andaman and Nicobar Islands, Maharashtra Arunachal Pradesh, Bihar, Chandigarh, Chhattisgarh, Delhi, Haryana, Himachal Pradesh, Jharkhand, Madhya Pradesh, Rajasthan, Uttar Pradesh and Uttarakhand
Kannada	Karnataka
Kashmiri	Jammu and Kashmir
Konkani	Goa, Karnataka, Maharashtra
Maithili	Bihar
Malayalam	Kerala, Andaman and Nicobar Islands, Lakshadweep
Manipuri	Manipur
Marathi	Dadra and Nagar Haveli, Daman and Diu, Goa, Maharashtra
Nepali	Sikkim, West Bengal
Oriya	Orissa
Punjabi	Chandigarh, Delhi, Haryana, Punjab
Santhali	Bihar, Chattisgarh, Jharkhand, Orissa
Sindhi	Parts of Mumbai, Gujarat and Rajasthan
Tamil	Tamil Nadu, Andaman and Nicobar Islands, Kerala, Puducherry
Telugu	Andaman and Nicobar Islands, Andhra Pradesh
Urdu	Andhra Pradesh, Delhi, Jammu and Kashmir, Uttar Pradesh

ETHNIC AND CULTURAL DIVISIONS

'Unity in Diversity' is the phrase popularized by one of India's early prime ministers to describe the harmony in the many divisions of India. To say India has serious divisions is not an exaggeration. Neighbouring China has a country with one official language written in one script, peopled by one ethnic group for the most part and administered by one federal government in Beijing. India has 22 official languages written in 13 scripts, is peopled by at least seven races and is ruled from a federal setup of 28 states. India has divisions on many lines:

- religion (Hindu vs. Muslim);
- geographical (north vs. south);

- caste (upper caste vs. lower caste);
- ethnicity (Aryan vs. Dravidian);
- location (urban vs. rural);
- exposure to modernity (English-speaking vs. non-English speaking).

Caste is a unique Indian institution, little understood by foreigners. Castes are large family or tribal units which had historically followed one profession, observe similar cultural practices, have one religious head and within which people marry. Government practises affirmative action (called reservation in India) in educational institutions and government jobs to help the backward and scheduled castes, and this evokes considerable ire amongst those who are not included. When the government recently mandated that the private sector also reserve seats for castes, it was widely criticized in the press. With the reduced clout of truly national parties, caste-based and religion-based parties have become central to national power. People of northern, western, and eastern India speak a language of the Indo-Aryan family tracing its origin to Sanskrit. People of southern India speak one of the four Dravidian languages, but they are also influenced by Sanskrit. Attempts to impose Hindi as the national language of India have been met with resistance from the southern states, especially Tamil Nadu, where parties which glorify a mythical Dravidian past have been in power for the past 40 years.

While most of those advocating ideas that may seem to exacerbate division are happy to work within the system, some of these have spawned actual secessionist movements. A few states in the northeastern part of India – which is culturally and geographically distant from Indian heartland – continue to have separatist movements. The Muslim-majority state of Kashmir is disputed by Pakistan and has an independence movement. Secessionist movement in the Sikh-dominated state of Punjab however has been pacified by clever policies.

Winston Churchill was incorrect when he called India a mere geographical expression. Along with the acknowledged geographical unity, India has too great a cultural, emotional, religious unity to splinter apart.

CLIMATE IN INDIA

India is a country that has a reputation for being hot and sunny. While this can certainly be true, the climate is subject to seasonal variations, and unsurprisingly for such a large country there are geographical and topographical variations, too. While European countries and most of the USA have four distinct seasons, in much of India the distinction is not so clear and there is summer, winter and the 'rainy season'. Typically the coolest part of the year will be around December to January, when temperatures as low as 16 to 20°C may be experienced even in southern Indian cities like Bangalore. However, after this brief cooler period, temperatures can mount quickly between February and March, giving some extremely warm weather between March and May with temperatures in the high 30s. In relatively cooler cities such as Bangalore, the temperatures may range from a typical 32 to perhaps 37°C. Bangalore formerly had a reputation as a 'garden city' and a favourite location for the British colonists, with a relatively cool climate resembling a warm summer day in the UK because the city is some 900 metres above sea-level.

While Bangalore is still a tolerable city to live in, the depletion of greenery and unimaginable increase in traffic pollution mean that it can no longer be regarded as having the cooler climate of a hill station, as would the southern Indian town of Ooty, for example, or the northern Indian mountain resort, Shillong. Other cool southern Indian towns that benefit from a high elevation include Coimbatore and the resort of Ercaud, near Salem in Tamil Nadu. However, fewer foreigners are likely to find employment in these cool and cloudy hill stations, although they make a nice place for a day out away from the hot weather. The city of Hyderabad is renowned for dreadfully hot weather in the two hottest months of the year, with temperatures as high as 45°C. Sometimes water shortages may occur at this difficult time of year.

Another city synonymous with heat is Chennai (Madras), which foreigners are advised against travelling to in the worst of the summer heat. However, from October until January these cities are quite tolerable, with temperatures ranging from perhaps the mid-30s in October, down to the high 20s at the coolest. With a sun-hat and some sun-cream in October, even in Chennai, visitors should be able to manage for up to an hour or more outdoors.

By November the climate can be quite comfortable and may even resemble an English or north-European summer's day. Curiously, despite its reputation for dryness, Chennai has suffered major floods in November (notably in 2003) and whether this represents an isolated anomaly or a change in weather patterns, remains to be seen. Being a coastal town, Chennai also fell victim to the tsunami of 2004.

In general, travel by road or rail is inadvisable from March to September, because the hottest months of the Indian year fall within this period.

While the popular image of India is one of sunshine, and undoubtedly the subcontinent is blessed with a lot of sunny weather, it also has its fair share of overcast or downright cloudy weather, especially in the monsoon (or rainy) season. Some states, such as the coastal region of Kerala, Goa, Maharashtra and Karnataka, are synonymous with water. The waterways of Kerala might be compared with the canals of Venice. It is not surprising that such regions are often extremely damp and humid. Coastal regions of Orissa and West Bengal are also subject to the capricious effects of coastal storms and cyclones, and flooding can occur at their fringes. On the opposite coast from Orissa and West Bengal, the city of Mumbai (Bombay) in Maharashtra was brought to a standstill by a prodigious tropical storm in 2005. While extreme conditions may prevail on the coast, inland the greatest problem is heat. Kolkata in West Bengal is relatively hot, while farther north, Delhi is a city of extremes, with temperatures ranging from perhaps 40°C down to zero.

When the Indians talk about the rainy season, it really comes in two major instalments. The first makes its way across the country in June to July time, bringing heavy rain, then there is a let-up in the weather before the receding monsoon brings rain back across the country in the opposite direction from September to perhaps October or November. These dates are somewhat variable and there may be some years in which the rains fail, or are disappointing. During this period there may not always be torrential rain but, on most days at least, there will be one sharp downpour which may often come at a fairly regular time.

While the rain is heavy and an umbrella most welcome, more often than not it will be over in half an hour to an hour and is rapidly dried up by the sunshine. The rains are really refreshing and lift the humidity at very stifling times of the year.

While the foreigner in India may well work in an air-conditioned environment, forays into offices in which a ceiling fan is the only source of climate control will be inevitable. During the worst times of year government or shop workers who do not benefit from air-conditioning may take a long lunch-break, or sometimes what even amounts to a siesta. Small shops may even close from lunchtime until perhaps 3 or 4 pm if the temperature is too uncomfortable, but they compensate by staying open until 9 or 10 pm. In some cities, like Bombay or Chennai, you will even find shops that do business through the night, avoiding the worst heat of the day.

Average temperatures in major Indian cities °C												
	Winter (Jan – Feb)			Summer (Mar – May)			Monsoon (Jun – Sep)			Post-monsoon (Oct – Dec)			Year-round
City	Min	Avg	Max	Min	Avg	Max	Min	Avg	Max	Min	Avg	Max	Avg
Bangalore	17	22	27	22	27	32	20	23	26	18	22	25	23
Chennai	22	25	29	26	30	34	26	30	34	23	26	29	28
Kolkata	15	21	27	24	29	34	26	29	31	19	24	28	26
Mumbai	19	24	30	24	28	32	25	28	30	23	27	31	27
New Delhi	8	14	20	23	32	38	27	31	32	14	17	20	25

COURTS IN INDIA

India has a written Constitution and codified central and state law. The Indian legal system is based on British Law and English is the official language in High Courts and the Supreme Courts. Although, known for its judicial integrity, the Indian legal system has a huge backlog due to staff shortage. Currently, there are over two million cases pending in 18 High Courts and more than 200,000 cases pending in the Supreme Court.

On the civil side there are 'Courts of Small Causes' (small claims courts), above them the City Civil Courts and District Courts. On the criminal side there are Metropolitan Magistrates' Courts, above them Courts of Judicial Magistrates and then Sessions Courts.

There are also Industrial Courts, Family Courts, Cooperative Courts and various Tribunals. Then, there are High Courts in each of the states, and above all is the Supreme Court of India.

ECONOMY

Lately, India has become one of Asia's booming economies. This hasn't always been the case. About 20 years back there was 'Licence Raj' and tightly regulated socialist policies. Government policy of freeing industry from oppressive regulations and encouraging competition has yielded great dividends. Business-wise, India is opening up and international companies are investing in India. European and American companies which were hesitant to do business with India in the 80s and 90s are now investing heavily.

India's economy has beaten expectations by growing at an annual rate of 9.3% in the first three months of 2006. There are rising foreign exchange reserves of close to US$140 billion, a booming capital market with the popular 'Sensex' (index of Mumbai Stock Exchange) topping the majestic 15,000 mark, flowing foreign direct investment (FDI) close to US$8 billion, and a more than 20 per cent surge in exports.

Bangalore is one of the world's leading software centres. India's abundant educated workforce provides it with a competitive edge in the global software market.

The booming private sector now accounts for about 75% of its GDP. However, India has a serious public-sector budget deficit of nearly 10% of its GDP.

CURRENCY

The currency in India is the rupee (Rs). There are one hundred paise (p) to a rupee (Rs1 = 100p). Coins come in denominations of 10p, 25p and 50p. They are rarely used. Coins are also available in denominations of Rs1, Rs2 and Rs5. All coins bear the lion's head on one side, but have different flip-sides marking different occasions in Indian history. All coins, except the two rupee coins are circular in shape. Two rupee coins have eleven sides.

Notes come in denominations of Rs1 (blue), Rs2 (light red), Rs5 (green), Rs10 (orange-violet), Rs20 (red-orange), Rs50 (violet), Rs100 (blue-green at centre, brown-purple at two sides), Rs500 (olive and yellow) and Rs1,000 (pink). All rupee notes have a picture of Mahatma Gandhi on the front, but different images on the reverse side.

The diversity of the country is also reflected in the currency notes. Each rupee note has its amount written in 17 languages with English and Hindi on the front and 15 other regional languages on the back.

CHANGING MONEY

Changing money is no longer a wearisome process in India. There are plenty of private accredited foreign exchange bureaus and banks offering competitive rates. However, please note that smaller foreign exchange bureaus may refuse to change travellers' cheques. Check the exchange rate and any commission charges in advance. Private foreign exchange bureaus offer slightly better rates for larger denomination notes than the banks.

Do keep all your exchange receipts (encashment certificates) as they may be required for visa extensions and other formalities, as well as when you want to convert Indian rupees back at the end of your stay.

EXCHANGE RATES

The following is a brief guide to the current exchange rates. Please note that exchange rates are subject to change and fluctuate daily. For real time rates check on the web at www.reuters.co.uk/currencies.

Exchange rates (correct at 22 Nov 2007)
1 Euro = 58.26 Indian rupees
1 US Dollar = 39.29 Indian rupees
1 Canadian Dollar = 39.71 Indian rupees
1 British Pound = 80.47 Indian rupees
1 South African Rand = 5.76 Indian rupees
1 Singapore Dollar = 27.04 Indian rupees
1 Brazilian Real = 22 Indian rupees
1 Chinese Yuan (RMB) = 5.29 Indian rupees
1 Taiwan Dollar = 1.21 Indian rupees
1 Japanese Yen = 0.36 Indian rupees
1 Australian Dollar = 34.17 Indian rupees
1 New Zealand Dollar = 29.49 rupees
1 Danish Krone = 7.81 Indian rupees
1 Norwegian Kroner = 7.24 Indian rupees
1 Swedish Kroner = 6.24 Indian rupees
1 Swiss Franc = 35.59 Indian rupees
1 Thai Baht = 1.25 Indian rupees

TRANSFERRING AND RECEIVING MONEY

See Chapter 8.

CASH MACHINES AND ATMs

ATMs are not common, but are becoming popular in cities. At present there are about 20,000 ATMs in India (fewer than in the UK). Almost all the cards issued around the world can be used in the cash machines in India. However, ATMs belonging to small regional banks may not accept cards belonging to customers of other banks. ATMs in India charge a withdrawal fee. You'll be advised on screen before the withdrawal about the charges and you can cancel the transaction. Remember, your own bank may make charges for withdrawal overseas. Cash machines in India give out Rs100 and Rs500 notes. (See Chapter 8 for further information.)

CREDIT AND DEBIT CARDS

Credit and debit cards are becoming increasingly popular in India. The majority of shops in major towns and cities accept Visa and MasterCard – it is very rare to find a merchant that accepts one and does not accept the other. American Express, Diners Club, Maestro and Visa Electron are also widely accepted. Discover Cards are not accepted in India. Some shops insist on a minimum transaction amount of Rs250 if you are paying by credit or debit cards. You might be levied a foreign exchange transaction charge by your bank when using your card in India: check with your own bank before using them.

POST OFFICE SERVICES

India has one of the largest post office networks in the world with around 1,055,333 post offices around the country. Postal services in India operate under the brand name 'India Post' that is owned by the government.

Post Offices in India are open from 9 am to 5 pm, Monday to Friday, and 9 am to 12 noon on Saturday.

The Post Office also offers a parcel service for sending parcels around the world.

Standard postage for domestic letters in India is Rs5 for every 20 grams. Mail usually takes a couple of days to be delivered. Important letters within India can be sent by registered post where a signature is obtained on delivery and an acknowledgement sent to you. This service is ideal when you need to prove that the items were received. There is a registration fee of Rs17 on top of the postage.

Urgent letters to India and abroad can be sent by Speed Post. The service guarantees delivery anywhere in India by a notified time. Rates vary according to distance and weight.

Stamps can also be bought at a small premium at many outlets including most local shops, newsagents and supermarkets.

The Post Office also provides a range of other services, including:

- money and postal orders;
- public provident fund;
- payment of some bills;
- national savings certificates;
- Kissan Vikas Patra (savings certificate);
- savings bank account;
- monthly income scheme account;
- recurring deposit account;
- post boxes for mail receipt;
- international money transfer service – 'Western Union' service to send or receive money;
- mail holding service;
- redirection service when you move home;
- *poste restante* service is also offered at all main post offices. You can receive mail anywhere in India at a main post office convenient to your location.

Further details about India Post are available on the web at www.indiapost.gov.in.

INSURANCE

After liberalisation, private insurance companies are mushrooming around India offering competitive rates on health, home, travel, life and general insurance.

Major insurance companies in India are:

- Aviva Life Insurance;
- Bajaj Allianz;
- Birla Sun Life Insurance;
- HDFC Standard Life Insurance;
- ICICI Prudential;
- ING Vysya;
- Kotak Mahindra;
- LIC;
- Max New York Life Insurance;
- Metlife India Insurance;
- Reliance Life Insurance;
- SBI Life Insurance;
- Shriram Life Insurance;
- Tata AIG Life Insurance.

WATER

Access to clean drinking water is still a major problem in India and the World Bank estimates that nearly 21% of all communicable diseases in India are now due to its unsafe drinking water. You'll need to take certain precautions:

- drink bottled or mineral water during your stay initially – it is available everywhere;
- insist on bottled water when you are visiting restaurants;

- do not buy or drink water in plastic sachets from road side vendors;
- install a UV purifier system in your house.

ELECTRICITY

Electricity supply throughout India is 240 volts at 50 hertz. You may need a voltage converter of you have a device that does not accept the above. Plugs and sockets are of two types: two round pins or three round pins arranged in a triangle. Adapters are widely available in electrical goods shops.

TELEVISION AND DVD

Like the UK and most of Europe, the television system in India is PAL but many sets sold in India are multi platform. DVD players in India are now multi-region compatible. That means they will also play discs originally coded for countries within a specific region. But, do check with your electrical retailer to make sure you are buying the latest multi-region player.

SHOPPING

India is a shoppers' paradise and shopping in India is a wonderful experience. One can easily find quality clothes, fabrics, books, carpets, jewellery, handicrafts and electronic and consumer items at reasonable prices. Most of the international brands are available in India at comparatively low prices. Shopping centres and districts are vibrant and buzzing with activity. American style shopping malls are becoming increasingly popular. The majority of shops are open from 9 am to 9.30 pm. However, some shops may close for a couple of hours during the afternoon.

Supermarkets

The Indian retail industry is still disorganized, chaotic and highly competitive. The majority of Indians still shop for food, produce and groceries at open markets, roadside vegetable vendors, street cart vendors and at small local shops. A visit to the local vegetable market is a memorable experience. Noisy and colourful, these markets have plenty of vegetable sellers sitting on the ground surrounded by an amazing variety of fresh vegetables and fruits. With a bag in hand, you move from one stall to another, stopping to examine the produce and to haggle a price (see the section on bargaining in Chapter 3).

However, supermarkets are beginning to appear in affluent areas of the cities. Reliance Fresh, Foodworld and Nilgiris are popular among the Indian middle classes. They, like Western supermarkets, stock a wide range of goods from ready-meals, to produce, to imported beer and spirits. However, they are expensive compared to open markets. Walmart and Tesco are due to open stores in India soon.

LAUNDRY

Private laundry facilities can be found all around town. Laundries offer collection and delivery of clothes at home. The cost of washing and ironing clothes is extremely reasonable. Laundries also offer dry cleaning and alteration facilities.

ALCOHOL

Alcohol availability depends on the state you are in. Some states like Goa and Karnataka are extremely relaxed, while states like Kerala, Andhra Pradesh, Gujarat and Haryana had prohibition until recently.

All around India, alcohol can be purchased from licensed 'Liquor shops' or 'Wine stores' (equivalent to an off-licence). They are open from 9 am to 10 pm. Foreign spirits and beer are available in India. However, they are slightly expensive compared to Indian brands. Indian-made Scotchstyle whisky is the most popular of distilled alcoholic spirits in India. These 'whisky' and other spirits in India are molasses based. Brand names of such Indian-made 'whisky' includes 'Bagpiper', 'Peter Scot' and 'McDowell's No. 1' reflect inspiration from Scotland.

Among local spirits that are available are the famous Goan 'Feni', 'Toddy' tapped out of palms trees and 'Arrack'. There are no age restrictions on purchase of alcohol or tobacco.

TIME

Despite its vastness, India has a single time zone. The standard time is Indian Standard Time with a time offset of UTC +5.30. India does not observe daylight-savings-time or any other seasonal adjustments.

Time differences	
Hawaii	IST – 15:30
Alaska	IST – 14:30
Pacific Time (US & Canada), Tijuana	IST – 13:30
Arizona	IST – 12:30
Mountain Time (US & Canada)	IST – 12:30
Central Time (US & Canada)	IST – 11:30
Mexico City, Tegucigalpa	IST – 11:30
Saskatchewan	IST – 11:30
Bogota, Lima, Quito	IST – 10:30
Eastern Time (US & Canada)	IST – 10:30
Indiana (East)	IST – 10:30
Atlantic Time (Canada)	IST – 09:30
Caracas, La Paz	IST – 09:30
Newfoundland	IST – 09:00
Brasilia	IST – 09:00
Buenos Aires, Georgetown	IST – 09:00
Greenwich Mean Time : Dublin, Edinburgh, London	IST – 05:30
Berlin, Stockholm, Rome, Bern, Brussels, Vienna	IST – 04:30
Lisbon	IST – 04:30
Paris, Madrid	IST – 04:30
Prague	IST – 04:30

Athens, Helsinki, Istanbul	IST – 03:30
Cairo	IST – 03:30
Eastern Europe	IST – 03:30
Harare, Pretoria	IST – 03:30
Israel	IST – 03:30
Baghdad, Kuwait, Nairobi, Riyadh	IST – 02:30
Moscow, St. Petersburg	IST – 02:30
Tehran	IST – 02:00
Abu Dhabi, Muscat, Tbilisi	IST – 01:30
Islamabad, Karachi	IST – 00:30
Almaty, Dhaka	IST + 00:30
Bangkok, Jakarta	IST + 02:00
Beijing	IST + 02:30
Hongkong, Perth, Singapore, Taipei	IST + 02:30
Tokyo, Osaka, Sapporo, Seoul, Yakutsk	IST + 03:30
Adelaide	IST + 04:00
Darwin	IST + 04:00
Brisbane, Melbourne, Sydney	IST + 04:30
Guam, Port Moresby, Vladivostok	IST + 04:30
Hobart	IST + 04:30
Magadan, Solomon Is, New Caledonia	IST + 05:30
Fiji, Kamchatka, Marshall Is	IST + 06:30
Wellington, Auckland	IST + 06:30

WEIGHTS AND MEASURES

India follows the metric system of measurement. Weights are quoted in kilograms and distances in kilometres. However, the Indian numbering system uses measurements in *crores* and *lakhs* (see the section on Indian English in Chapter 3).

TELEPHONE

The country code for India is 91. To dial another city or town you will first need to dial the regional code and then the number. To dial an international number dial 00 then the country code and then the phone number. A list of regional and international dialling codes is given in Appendix 1.

Public telephones

In India, manned and unmanned (payphone) public telephone facilities exist. However, manned public telephone facilities are popular and are referred to as Public Call Offices (PCOs). They offer local, STD (inter-city) and international call facilities. Some of them offer fax and internet facilities as well. The minimum call charge for a local call is Rs2. Call charges within India and abroad are cheaper between 10 pm and 8 am, during weekends and public holidays.

Non-geographic numbers

India now has certain non-geographic toll-free phone numbers. They are mainly used by commercial organizations with a national presence. The numbers are similar to the American system and begin with 1800.

Directory enquiries

The standard number for directory enquiries in India is 197 for local enquiries and 1583 for national enquiries. Directory enquiries are also available online at www.bsnl.co.in/onlinedirectory.htm.

Mobile phones

India has one of the fastest-growing mobile phone markets in the world. In India, like America, people usually say 'cell' or 'cellphone' rather than 'mobile' and 'SMS' rather than 'text-message'. Mobile phone rates are low and it is definitely worth having one whilst in India. The major networks are:

1. BSNL (www.bsnl.co.in/service/mobile.htm);

2. MTNL (www.mtnl.net.in);

3. Idea Cellular Ltd (www.ideacellular.com);

5. Reliance Telecom Ltd (www.ril.com);

6. Vodafone (www.vodafone.in);

7. Airtel (www.airtelworld.com);

8. Spice (www.spicemobile.in);

9. BPL Mobile Communications Ltd (www.bplmobile.com);

10. Escorts Telecommunications Ltd (www.escotelmobile.com).

You need to be aware of the network coverage in India. Most providers have good network coverage in all of the big cities and towns. However, one often finds that it is possible to receive calls but not make any (especially international) in some parts of towns. Rural India and smaller towns have limited coverage.

Getting a mobile phone connection is a slightly tiresome process in India if you are a foreigner. You'll have the option of going post-paid (contract) or prepaid (pay-as-you-go). Either way, you'll need to buy the phone outright in India. Phone prices vary depending on the handset you wish to purchase. You may wish to use an unlocked handset from your home country. Usually your company will provide one which is 'post-paid' and for which your bill will be deducted from your salary. You can ask for business calls to be excluded from the bill if you desire.

Post-paid offers slightly better call rates and you have the option of choosing the tariff plan. SIM cards are quite cheap and prices vary from about Rs200 to 250 depending on the network.

You can find stores selling mobile phones all around towns and cities. To get a SIM card you'll need to fill in the respective application and submit proof of identity and address and pay the required amount. The following documents are accepted as proof of identity:

- your passport with a valid Indian visa;

- your corporate ID card;

- your PAN card (see Chapter 6);

- your Indian driving licence.

For proof of address your residence permit, your utility bill or any document issued by central or state government or local bodies showing residential address is sufficient. The above requirement is mandatory for everyone in India. SIM cards usually take up to 24 hours to get activated.

With prepaid you'll need to be aware that if you are travelling around India, you may find it difficult to top-up the phone even with the same network provider. The value of recharge cards varies according to the service provider. In India, validity of the recharge varies according to the amount paid and not all the amount is carried towards the phone calls. For example, validity of a recharge card purchased at Rs335 will be 30 days and the actual call credit will be about Rs150. The validity of a recharge card purchased at Rs650 will be 45 days and the actual call credit will be around Rs350, and so on.

INTERNET

There are numerous 'cyber cafés' around major towns and cities in India that give you access to the internet for about 10 to 30 rupees an hour with additional charges for printing or scanning.

EMERGENCY SERVICES

India does not have one standard number for emergency services. Police, fire and ambulance service have three different toll-free numbers. Most hospitals offer quicker private ambulance services and the numbers are listed in Yellow Pages (see Chapter 10).

Emergency numbers in India
Police 100
Fire 101
Ambulance 102

POLICE

Police in India have a reputation of being rude, corrupt and incompetent. They are a law unto themselves and it is best to be over-respectful to the police, in which case they will treat you well. Policing in India is divided into several state police forces. Every state police force has its own website which contains useful information. You can find further details about the police service in your area at www.mha.nic.in/police_main. htm.

BEGGARS

India has a massive population of beggars and street children. You are bound to come across beggars and street children and be pestered by them. Beggars will often go as far as touching you, following you and tugging your clothes. It is best to ignore them or refuse loudly by saying 'No!' (this is what the local Indians do). Ask for assistance from local Indians if you get mobbed or followed by beggars.

You may wish to donate a few rupees to elderly or physically challenged people. If you wish to donate a few rupees, it is best to give them money at the time of leaving, otherwise you will run the risk of being mobbed by other beggars on the street. Generally a donation of Rs5 to Rs10 is appropriate.

MAPS

Political and geographical maps issued by the Geographical Survey of India are full of information to help you to get to know your local area, region, state and the country. These maps are available from most book stores.

The Indian equivalent to the Western-style A–Z street atlas is TTK Maps which should help you to get around towns and cities during your stay. TTK also publish maps of national roads, Indian railways, air routes and tourist guides. You can find further information and view maps online on their website at www.ttkmaps.com.

GAY AND LESBIAN LIFE

Homosexuality is a criminal offence in India and the rights of gays and lesbians are not recognized by the Indian judiciary or government. Police in India still harass gays and lesbians. The issue is not openly talked about by the majority of Indians.

However, there exists a large vibrant underground gay and lesbian nightlife in major cities including discos, parties and cruising areas. *Time Out* (Delhi) has a dedicated column covering gay events in Delhi every week.

The internet offers a meeting place for gays and lesbians with chatrooms and dating sites. These include www.GayDia.com, www.gaybombay. com, and in.guys4men.com which are popular among the gay dating scene and www.voicesagainst377.org and www.infosem.org which campaign on behalf of the gay and lesbian community.

DRUGS

Use of all hallucinogenic, psychotropic and narcotic drugs are strictly forbidden by law in India. Possession, production, transportation, supply and consumption of drugs will result in criminal conviction. The penalties are severe and range from imprisonment from 10 to 20 years for the first offence to 15 to 30 years for any subsequent offence.

WEAPONS

Possession of weapons, including replica weapons and knives is prohibited in India. Sentences are usually harsh and anyone found to possess one without a licence can be jailed for a minimum of five years and also be liable for a fine. Arms licences are only issued to citizens of India.

PUBLIC HOLIDAYS

Public holidays are quite common in India where every other day is auspicious on religious grounds. There are national public holidays in India for religious festivals, birthdays and remembrance days of its national heroes like Gandhi as well as several state holidays (depending on the state you live). Private organizations may continue to function on state holidays. Services during public holidays will be restricted, but transport services continue to run. There is a surcharge for taxis and autos.

National holidays in India for 2008
Dec/Jan* Bakrid (Muslim feast of sacrifice)
10 Jan Muharram (Muslim New Year)
26 Jan Republic Day
Feb* Mahashivratri (Night of Hindu God Shiva)
Feb/Mar* Mahavir Jayanthi (Birthday of Mahavir)
Mar/Apr* Milad-Un-Nabi (Birth of the Prophet)
21 Mar Good Friday
24 Mar Easter Monday
Apr/May* Buddha Purnima
15 Aug* Independence Day
Sep* Janmashtami (Lord Krishna's birthday)
Sep/Oct* Dussehra (Vijaya Dashami)
2 Oct Mahatma Ghandi's Birthday
2 Oct Id ul Fitr (End of Ramadan)
Nov* Deepavali or Diwali (Festival of Lights)
Nov* Guru Nanak's Birthday
25 Dec Christmas Day
26 Dec Boxing Day
29 Dec Muharram (Islamic New Year)
Dates need to be confirmed according to respective religious calendars

BUNDH (STRIKE)

Public strikes in the form of forced total shut down are quite common around India. They are usually called by the opposition political parties to protest against government policies. This form of protest may be restricted to a town/city, region or state or may be held nationally. They last for a day and shops, business establishments and banks may be closed. Transport services will also be severely restricted.

SAFETY

India is generally a safe country. However, you should take certain precautions to protect yourself and your valuables. Do not carry large sums of money on you or keep them in your place of residence. While travelling, be extra careful with luggage on overnight trains and buses. It is best not keep your wallet in your back pocket as pickpockets are common in public transport. Women are advised to avoid travelling alone at night. Avoid walking through dark alleys or poorly lit streets as there have been instances of mugging.

There have been reports where unsuspecting foreign businesspeople and their families have been targeted for kidnapping. If you have a meeting with a potential client or an unknown individual, it is best to meet in a public place. Do keep your contacts at home and in India well informed of your whereabouts and activities. Also, keep copies of your important travel documents in an accessible place.

Avoid Kashmir and the northeastern states of India as they have serious terrorism problems. Naxalite (Maoist) problems are common in rural Bihar and Andhra Pradesh.

3
Life in India

SPORTS

Sports are not given a high priority in India, but of those that are played cricket is dominant followed by hockey, tennis and football. Facilities are limited and generally in poor condition. Cricket, football and basketball are often played on the streets or in small public parks or grounds where air pollution is a major problem. India's awful record in the Olympics and other international games is a clear indication that sports are not given a high priority in Indian life. Public swimming pools in most of the cities and towns are often overcrowded and unhygienic. Hill walking and trekking societies do exist, but they are often more for amusement than exercise. Private gyms are mushrooming in big cities. Some large companies also have gym facilities on site.

THE SOCIAL SCENE

The social scene in India is a little different from in the West, but perhaps less so as the affluence of the emerging Indian middle class continues to expand. While many countries count football (soccer) as their most popular sport, and the Americans enjoy baseball and American football, Indians are fanatical about cricket. Whether this means watching the match on television, discussing the state of play with friends, attending a cricket match or playing for a local side oneself, the importance of cricket cannot be underestimated.

Along with cricket, India's other great obsession is watching movies. Traditionally cinemas are located in every part of town, but although this is still the case, sometimes Western blockbusters can only be seen in multiplexes or malls that may be a long distance away. An alternative that is now impacting on the film industry, is the home or office viewing of DVDs and VCDs, which are often pirated and sold on street-corners. By fair means or foul, a group of Indian friends will find a way to see the latest hit movies.

While many young Britons socialize by pubbing and clubbing, these activities are not as widespread in India. Cafés, pubs and clubs can definitely be found in affluent Indian cities, where a sizeable segment of the young have a 'modern' outlook. However, they are not as well-accepted as in the West. The bars tend to be mainly clustered in certain sections of the city, rather than being widely distributed around town, as they are in British cities. However, you will frequently encounter small 'liquor-shops' which reveal that India also has a drink problem, and these tend to service the city's winos and errant husbands. From a traditional and respectable point of view, Indians tend to view the drinking of alcohol as immoral. While the British regard students having a drink to be generally harmless and good-natured, Indians (especially Indian women) are quite frightened to see drinking and it is not so widespread (at least openly) amongst the middle-aged. The drinking and clubbing phenomenon is more prevalent amongst single software engineers (usually male) and other youngsters who may be living a long way from their families, and who have their own disposable income, such as some call-centre workers. However, this *demi-monde* does not sit comfortably with traditional Indian values, and as a result bachelors are often excluded from apartment blocks.

A much more common social event for Indians is simply eating out. A group of students or workers will book a table at one of a wide number of restaurants. Indian women may wear a saree specially for the evening, while men may wear a smart shirt. The person who has invited everyone (perhaps for their birthday) will usually pay, which is referred to as giving a 'treat'. In terms of organization, the group will arrange to meet at a certain time, for example 7:30 pm, but in reality it will end up being

8:30 pm (IST, or Indian Standard Time). During and after dinner photos will be taken and a great time will be had by all.

Restaurants in India do very good business and are far busier than in Britain. Another popular activity is shopping, and friends will readily hop in an autorickshaw or a taxi to go to the shops and possibly enjoy some *chaats* (snack items such as *pav bhaji*, *bhel puri* or *pani puri*) at the same time. Depending on your location and social circle, this activity may involve a trip to a modern shopping mall with an ice-cream parlour, coffee-shop or McDonalds. In India some shops may close during the hot part of the afternoon, but they more than compensate by staying open until 9:30 pm, making Indian cities vibrant and buzzing with activity.

A common alternative day out is for a group of friends to share the cost of a van and driver, and take a trip to the countryside for 'trekking' or seeing some location of outstanding natural beauty, such as a hill station or the confluence of two rivers. A picnic lunch may be organized, lots of photos will be taken and everyone will return home in the van late in the afternoon, tired but happy.

While single Indians are very sociable, this gregariousness is necessarily reduced after marriage and, although married couples will still attend group dinners at a nice restaurant, they may not always accept an invitation to a movie. Instead, married Indians will be happy to invite you to their house for a home-cooked dinner, or perhaps to attend a family religious function, if you show you are interested. In fact, inviting friends to meet one's family can be regarded as another social activity.

Strangely, when a group of friends decide to go to the temple, this can also feel like a social event. Temples sometimes have their own shops and eateries can be close by, so provided you share an interest in religious matters you can socialize in this way too!

'TREATS' AND HOME INVITATIONS

Quite often Indians will find any reason to suggest that a friend should 'give a treat' of sweets or a meal. This is very common amongst friends and is a very natural part of the familiarity of Indian culture. Expect to be invited home, where your hosts will be anxious that you should not leave the household hungry. Usually guests are honoured by being served first, so don't feel uncomfortable that your hosts may not be eating with you. Written invitations are not required and are regarded as an example of excessive formality. Eat (and hand over money) with your right hand, but drink with your left (this is slightly flexible with drinking). One thing that is quite difficult for the British, is to stop saying 'Please' and 'Thank you' when speaking to Indians, who regard these marks of British good manners as a sign of a formal distance inappropriate to friendship. In an informal situation, Indians may share a bottle when imbibing a soft drink. However, there is no need to worry, as mouths do not touch the bottle, and the drink is poured from an inch or two above each person's mouth. This is something of an acquired skill.

EXPATRIATE SOCIAL SCENE

You'll come across expatriate societies in major cities. In Chennai there is even an American Expatriate Wives' Association that publishes a journal and has regular meetings where topics are discussed about safety in India, how to treat the Indian servants, where to buy the best clothes, holding charity sales, and so on.

The US embassy in India has a list of American expatriate associations in India and their contact details. Several other embassies have listings of their nationality's expatriate association in India. You can find information about your nationality groups at www.meetup.com or at www.expatindia.com.

INDIAN FILMS

Indian films are as much a part of Indian life as spicy food, tea or cricket, and are something which you are sure to encounter during your stay in the subcontinent. You will recognize the faces of Indian movie stars even if you never see an Indian film because these engaging personalities grace the screens of India's TVs every 15 minutes advertising everything from motorbikes and credit cards to soft drinks and toothpaste! On the streets of Indian cities massive posters ensure that you will be aware of the latest Hindi and local-language movies, and top stars lend their endorsements to Coca Cola, Pepsi, or major mobile phone contractors, such as India's Air-Tel.

Now the Hindi movie industry (known affectionately as 'Bollywood' from 'Bombay Hollywood') has really gone global and you may have already seen some subtitled Hindi movies in the West, or have friends who are enthusiasts. One of the top Hindi movie stars, Aishwarya Rai Bachchan, is a model for watches, soaps and creams, and can be seen on posters in UK shop displays and occasionally in British television advertisements. Some of the most popular Hindi movie stars, like actor Amitabh Bachchan are even exhibited as waxworks in Madame Tussaud's in London.

A typical Bollywood plot

At first, Indian movies may be a little difficult to appreciate, resembling Western pantomimes and musicals as much as they do mainstream English language films. Often the characters' qualities are exaggerated, with sugary-sweet heroines, glaringly evil baddies and kindly mothers. Family values are paramount and typically a young man (who may be from a poor background) has to struggle to prove his worthiness for the hand of a girl whose rich parents disapprove of him. In the process villains must be vanquished, friendships and love triangles formed, and birthday parties may be held for children, with a sprinkling of funerals and weddings thrown in for good measure. The action may be set in a college, a historical setting, the criminal underworld of Bombay or an affluent Western country, but the formula for a successful movie or 'super-hit' should not stray too far from these conventions. The one indispensable part of the equation is to include a number of catchy song-and-dance routines in the movie, with a beautiful heroine and a dashing hero (occasionally the hero may still sometimes be too old and overweight in a south Indian movie!).

While the Hindi stars are becoming internationally famous, the level of movie star mania in southern India reaches even more bizarre extremes to the point where the funerals of stars (notably the Tamil movie star, M.G.R., M.G. Ramachandran) may be accompanied by rioting, with ensuing deaths. There is even a striking memorial building dedicated to M.G.R. at the side of Marina Beach in Chennai (Madras), which befits a national hero! Another Tamil movie superstar, Rajnikant has an enormous fan-following and people have committed suicide just because they couldn't get a ticket to one of his movies! If you are working in the city of Hyderabad, you will find that the regional language of Telugu also has its own superstars, with the actor Cheeranjeevi being the current favourite.

Indian movie songs have the same kind of status in India that pop songs have in the West and dominate the airwaves on the radio. You will soon find yourself humming or singing along to these catchy tunes, even if you don't understand the words!

Indian movies (at least the ones with less dialogue) are often so easy to follow that you can understand what is going on even without any subtitles. However, if you make a little effort you will soon find you are recognising the Hindi words for such staples as 'heart' (*dil*), 'love' (*pyaar*), or 'liar' (*joot*), that turn up in almost every movie. It is really well worth going to watch some Hindi or local language movies with your Indian friends. Not only will you gain an important insight into Indian culture, but you will be able to discuss the perennial subject of who is the best actor, or actress, and why. This is tantamount to discussing who is the best footballer in the premier league and will always draw a lively discussion!

INDIAN MUSIC

Indian music is one of the most distinctive aspects of Indian culture, as evocative of the Indian experience as the spicy food or the colourful Indian clothing. Indian music is also highly accessible, and you will soon find yourself humming the latest hit tunes, which tend to be generated by the movie industry, rather than by pop stars (although there is a growing Indian rock and pop industry, with reality TV shows fuelling this trend). Your Indian friends and colleagues are sure to have a favourite movie music director or composer, and 'playback' singer and will be as happy to discuss the subject of music as they are the latest cricket scores.

Many of these composers and especially the singers are well-recognized media figures in their own right, such as composer A. R. Rahman, 'The Mozart from Madras' who has worked with Andrew Lloyd Webber. There are the evergreen singers Asha Bhosle (who has sung with Robbie Williams, Boy George and Michael Stipe) and Lata Mangeshkar, who featured in the Guinness Book of Records over many years for her sheer volume of music sales. Other current favourites include the near-perfect voices of female singers Kavita Krishnamurthy, Alka Yagnik and Sunidhi Chauhan. Amongst the males, you will soon become familiar with the handsome heart-throb singer Sonu Nigam, the warm and sometimes humourous songs of Adnan Sami (actually born in Britain of mixed Pakistani and Indian parentage) and the legendary Tamilian composer of hits Ilayaraaja, to name but a few.

Many of the favourites like the sisters, Asha and Lata, are now old ladies, and the three favourite male movie singers, Mohammed Rafi, Mukesh and Kishore Kumar are sadly no longer with us. Nevertheless, their appeal is eternal and their songs live on. Age seems to be less of an issue in Indian music than in the West, and stars of all ages share popularity. In the same way you will notice that Western 1970s groups such as Boney M, Abba, Jethro Tull and The Eagles are still widely played in India, together with the latest chart hits.

You may already be familiar with Indian music from the *sitar* and *tabla* performances in BBC cultural programmes, soundtracks in Indian restaurants or even excerpts of Indian music in Hollywood movies (*Bulletproof Monk*, *Inside Man*, *Dead Man Walking*). Furthermore, Punjabi Bhangra music has now filtered into the Western consciousness and even created a sub-genre of rap music. However, the true picture of Indian music is much more vast and impressive than anything you have heard in the West, with a tradition stretching back thousands of years. Most of what we in the West regard as Indian music is in the northern 'Hindustani' style.

A different, '*Carnatic*' style, coming from the south of India is equally important, developing from India's sacred music, with a strong emphasis on vocals. There is also a much wider range of musical instruments in Indian music than the *sitars* and *tablas* we are aware of in the West. The *mridangam* (a kind of horizontal drum), *veena* (a classical string instrument) and the *santoor*, are southern Indian alternatives to the northern Indian *tabla* (small vertical drums) and *sitar* (northern Indian string instrument made famous by Ravi Shankar and used by Beatle, George Harrison in the song, *Norwegian Wood*). Another important Indian instrument, especially in the north, is the *santoor*, a wooden board with around 70 strings stretched out for plucking with special mallets. This instrument, which was brought to India by the Persians, creates a highly ambient, atmospheric sound which you can hear at concerts given by world experts such as Pandit Shivkumar Sharma.

When you hear Indian music it will recall your memories of India and her ancient culture for the rest of your life. You will soon find yourself adding your favourite Indian music (*sangeet*) to your CD and MP3 collection, because you want to bring the tunes (*raagas*), beats (*taals*) and songs (*ghanas*) back to your home country!

THE MEDIA IN INDIA

Democratic India has a long tradition of a free and colourful media. While newspapers around the world are faced with falling sales, the cheap newspapers of India are seeing a continued boom: a Price Waterhouse study forecasts sales to be nearly 100 billion US dollars in 2011. The habit of beginning the day with a newspaper is forgotten elsewhere, but is very much alive in India. Cable television in India is relatively cheap too, with 100 channels costing a mere 3 dollars a month to the subscribers. Indian papers have a daily circulation of over 50 million, with 23 million in the Hindi language alone. India has 40 domestic news agencies, over 45,000 newspapers, 7,000 cable channels and 33,000 local cable operators. While Indian newspapers give ample space to stories of Indian film and cricket stars and astrology; they consistently devote more columns to foreign news than papers of other countries.

English newspapers in India sometimes use words and phrases that seem to an outsider as either delightfully quaint or incomprehensible. All major cities have two or more English newspapers and more local language (vernacular) papers. There are morning newspapers, afternoon newspapers and evening newspapers. India has national newspapers with editions from various cities: some of the famous newspapers are *The Hindu*, *Times of India*, *The Hindustan Times*, *The Indian Express* and *The Statesman*.

Doordarshan 1 and Doordarshan 2 (which literally means 'far viewing') are the government run free television terrestrial channels. Unfortunately, these show very little worth watching and often have a weak signal. However, for a small monthly payment (about 200–300 rupees) you can get lots of cable channels, with BBC World, Star News, CNN International and Australian news in English, as well as Hollywood movies and documentaries on HBO, Star Movies, National Geographic and Discovery Channel. Of course the majority of channels are broadcast in Hindi and the major regional languages.

With just 200 ISPs and 3.5 million subscribers, the internet in India may not have seen the penetration experienced elsewhere, but has grown 11 times over the last seven years. The dotcom investigative news websites have made news recently with their sensational exposés of corruption. Censorship for obscenity and ethical violation is carried out by the Press Council of India, a statutory body with representatives of the press and government, paid for by the press.

DISCRIMINATION

Indian society is very hierarchical, with distinctions of caste, gender, financial status, educational background and regional identity. In some ways, as a foreigner you are in the fortunate position of side-stepping many of the usual Indian categorizations. Indians are generally very thoughtful and considerate and the most common form of discrimination you will encounter will be positive discrimination, whereby a foreigner will be given extra help and understanding.

Having said this, you may occasionally come across some unexpected stereotyping of foreigners. The colonial domination of India by the British is still fresh in the minds of many Indians. Because of this, you may sometimes come across an insecure individual who regards you as a

'Britisher' who bears full responsibility for all of his country's woes. Curiously, Indians seem to have a soft spot for the French (whose colonies in India were overwhelmed by the British) and are often keen to learn the French language and culture.

Caucasians are sometimes stereotyped as rich and selfish (but disciplined and hard-working), loose and immoral (the 'free' Western lifestyle is maligned, but secretly envied by some of the more chauvinistic gents). Westerners all get divorced (pronounced 'die-vorced' in India), do not eat spicy or vegetarian food and don't care about their families. Occasionally you may hear discriminatory remarks about Afro-Caribbeans and Chinese! The Japanese are regarded with a sense of awe, while America is a highly desirable place to work, but is frequently maligned as a bastion of 'Western immorality'.

A form of discrimination which is more blatant is Islamophobia, constantly stoked by the relationship with India's neighbour, Pakistan. However, it is quite likely that you will never be troubled by any of these stereotypes, for Indians are very open-minded and always interested to learn about other cultures and strike up a friendship. The warmth of Indian hospitality and the friendliness of an Indian welcome for visitors from overseas is one of the country's most endearing qualities.

BRIBERY AND CORRUPTION

It is often said that India is a corrupt country, or that in the Indian subcontinent there is a culture of bribery. However, this is perhaps to misunderstand a culture in which almost everything is flexible or negotiable to a certain degree and outright bribery is only the extreme end of the spectrum.

Corruption is certainly a problem recognized by the Indian people, and on one day each year Indian workers in government institutions must stop work for a few minutes to swear a vow of vigilance against corruption. Many Indian movies have highlighted the problems in society caused not only by corrupt politicians and officials, but also by private individuals. It is also common to hear Indians blame corruption for the decline of Indian civilization, and it is widely appreciated that the resulting vulnerability left the subcontinent open to colonial exploitation.

Because the problem of bribery is so well-recognized, if you do come across it, it may be in the form of a request for a 'gift'. If the official is unsatisfied with the size of the 'gift' you may have to repeat the process. This is one of the reasons why it is better to bring an Indian friend along when meeting officials in case you need some help in handling the 'negotiation'. It is also common for bribes or gifts to be requested by officials or middlemen whose signatures are necessary when starting any kind of business proposition. Some businesspeople may choose to give a small gift pre-emptively (which would be regarded as an illegal sweetener in the West) to reduce the chance of a bribe being requested, thereby reinforcing the culture of corruption.

BARGAINING

Another aspect of Indian life that is closely related to corruption is the culture of bargaining when shopping. Do not be surprised to be charged a 'foreign' price for goods that is much higher than the one charged to Indians, because 'you are a rich foreigner'.

Expect merchants to try to cheat you, but if you regard it as a game and smile at the outrageous prices, you will soon understand another aspect of Indian culture – negotiation. Watch your Indian friends turn their backs and start walking away from a salesman's cheeky prices (sometimes the vendor will immediately start shouting lower rates apologetically). Of course, you cannot always have an Indian friend at your side, but you will soon learn roughly what the correct prices for various items should be. With this knowledge in hand you can engage or disengage from a negotiation at will and if you have no intention of buying, don't even bother making eye contact with the salesman and just walk on!

INDIAN ENGLISH

What is Indian English?

One of the factors which makes India so attractive to foreigners and foreign businesses is the widespread use of the English language within the subcontinent. In fact, India has now edged in front of America as the country with the largest English-speaking population. However, you will soon find out that the Indian version of English is quite distinct from other varieties, such as British, American, Australian, or Caribbean English. In fact, it may take a few days for some of your Indian colleagues to understand your 'accent'. While there is no need to speak slowly and patronisingly, if you have a natural tendency to speed up when talking excitedly, try to remember that it may be hard for your friends to follow. There is still some controversy over whether Indian English is a condensation of local vocabulary, pronunciation and grammatical tics, or a dialect. There are many Indians who learn the grammar of standard English to a much higher level than British schoolchildren. Nevertheless, when you live and work in India, Indian English is an inescapable fact of life, so we have devoted a few paragraphs to this subject.

Indian English is now a subject of great interest, with numerous articles available on the subject. Try not to think of your own version of English as the correct one, and the Indian version / versions as 'wrong', but rather as a different and creative way of expressing oneself. Indian English is a fascinating creative combination of old English expressions from colonial times, grammatical constructions and direct translations from the native speaker's language, words borrowed from other colonial languages, and especially Indian languages such as Hindi, together with simplifications of English grammar that increase the user-friendliness of the language. You may even find yourself picking up some Indian words or expressions and using them when you go back home, as the British colonists did when they brought home the words 'bungalow, pyjamas, shampoo, chutney, pundit and chintz' which became firmly lodged in the English language.

Expressing quantity

Grammatical differences you will notice include different ways of expressing quantity, where a British Indian speaker would say, for example, 'Could you give me some help', in India one might say, 'Could you give me one help', or even, 'One help you give me' (word order is altered to resemble that in an Indian language). Another example is provided by the word 'news', for which the British speaker would use 'some' or 'a piece of', while the Indian speaker may not, e.g. 'Another happy news of making investment is that interest rate has risen'. In British English we might say, 'Some more good news for investors is that the interest rate has risen', or 'Another piece of good news for investors is that the interest rate has risen'. You will find many more examples when you hear Indian English.

Although it doesn't cause any real confusion, Indians may express that something is a small amount, by saying 'less' or 'very less' – 'Was your *tiffin* (breakfast) enough, or less?'.

There is a distinctly different use of the articles, 'a' and 'the' in Indian English, again reflecting the difficulty in translating directly from an Indian language into English. The indefinite article 'a' is often omitted, for example: 'Deduction of interest on loan would be allowed', whereas the British speaker might say, 'Deduction of interest on a loan would be allowed'. The definite article, 'the' is often also omitted.

Like the Spanish speaking English, Indians will often over-correct and add 'the' when it would not be required in British English, e.g. 'With this knowledge, you are free from the worry' is an Indian form of 'With this knowledge you are free from worry'.

The present participle, perhaps especially in southern India, is used out of context (compared to British English). For example, 'She is loving him' may be used in Indian English, where a British speaker would simply say, 'She loves him'.

The word 'only' is over-used, and is often used to give extra emphasis to a sentence. For example, 'Do not cheat us, we are from here only' (meaning, 'Don't cheat us, this is our hometown and we know how things work around here'), or 'It is me only' (which doesn't mean, 'Just me', but is closer to, but not exactly, 'It's me, of course!' in British English), and 'Do it like this only', which is something like 'Do it this way!' in British English, but the word 'only' is about one third to one half as emphatic as an exclamation mark.

Redundant words

In Indian English you will find that words that would not be required in British English are often included to more clearly emphasize a point. For example, instead of 'This is called a microphone', you may hear, 'This is called as a microphone'. Perhaps this is a hybridization of sentences using 'called', which does not require 'as', with sentence constructions which do, when you would use, 'referred to as' or 'known as'.

Plurals

Indian English often does not deal with plurals in the same way as British English, so nouns which would already be regarded as plural by a British speaker may be double pluralized in Indian English, for example, 'We need to buy these equipments' instead of 'We need to buy these pieces of equipment'. This illustrates the point that Indians sometimes make, that the Indian English version is more concise! As an extreme example of this double pluralization, 'sockses' is often heard as a plural for 'sock'. Curiously, you will also find cases in which pluralization does not take place. For instance, if someone suggests you buy trousers, they might say, 'One pant you take' to mean, 'Why not buy a pair of trousers?' or 'Go on, buy a pair of trousers'. Similarly, 'a pair of scissors' may become 'one scissor' in Indian English.

Words for family members

In India, extended families are very important, and many descriptions, like 'cousin', 'aunt' or 'uncle' are insufficiently precise. In Indian English you will hear 'cousin-brother' to mean male cousin and 'cousin-sister' to mean female cousin. However, with the traditional closeness of the extended family, an Indian may also use the words 'brother' or 'sister' to describe a cousin. Other members of the family, such as maternal and paternal aunts and uncles, older and younger sisters and brothers, as well as male and female in-laws have very specific terms in Indian languages and these are intermingled freely with English.

It must be noted that 'uncle' and 'aunty' are also used politely to address someone old enough to be your father or mother. This may be when you visit a friend's family for the first time, or even when meeting a stranger, if you want to be polite, but friendly (but make sure that the age difference between yourself and the person you address is great enough!).

'It's all a cultural misunderstanding!'

Sometimes when referring to people who are not quite as close as a friend, even if they are colleagues one has worked with, Indians may say 'those people', for example 'I haven't had any contact from those people'. The word 'fellow', which is now slightly outmoded in British English, is still very popular in India. This means that a highly regarded young man may be described as a 'terrific fellow'. Sometimes an Indian may say, 'you people' to mean 'foreigners', in a way which would not be derogatory as a direct translation from Hindi, but certainly would not be used in polite British English.

In Indian English one may emphasize a sense of urgency by repeating a word. For example, if you have ordered a cup of black coffee (referred to as 'decoction' or 'decoction only') and even after you have asked, no sugar has been brought after a minute or two, you may go to the counter and say, 'Sugar, sugar' with a sense of urgency, saying the two words in rapid succession while making eye contact with the waiter. While this could be construed as rude in British English, lacking as it does, 'please', and seeming rather pushy, it is perfectly acceptable in Indian English.

Sometimes in Indian English, a very direct way of giving or requesting advice is used. It may come in the form of commands which would not be culturally acceptable in British English, but are quite acceptable in

70

India, perhaps because of its hierarchical society. An Indian may say, 'You do one thing', then provide a suggestion, whereas a British speaker might say, 'You could try ...' before making the same suggestion.

Differences in vocabulary

'Roaming' can be used to refer to a young lady undertaking social events such as shopping or watching a film at the cinema without her father's knowledge or permission.

Indians use the American word, 'movie', rather than the British, 'film' for a show at the cinema. However, paradoxically, what a British person would call a 'blue movie' (i.e. an offensively explicit movie) would be called a 'blue film' in India. Incidentally, the word 'cinema' is not used, but instead, one goes to see a movie at the 'theatre'. Moreover, if the film you want to see is sold out and you can only buy tickets from touts, these are referred to as 'black' tickets, rather than 'black market' tickets in British English. These tickets are said to be bought 'in black'.

In India the word 'since' can be used to mean 'for' when expressing a period of time. Examples of this usage are 'I haven't mailed you since a long time' and 'Since how long have you been in India?'.

While the British use a 'ruler' to measure an object's length in centimetres or inches, Indians use a 'scale'. For example, to ask, 'Is there a ruler?' in Indian English one might hear, 'Scale is there?'. The word 'rowdy' is usually an adjective in British English, in Indian English it is commonly used as an adjectival noun to describe a trouble-maker or hooligan.

'Kitty party' is an expression used for a girls-only event, roughly corresponding to a British 'coffee-morning' or 'girls' night-out'.

Lakhs and crores

While the British and Americans tenaciously hold on to 'miles', in favour of 'kilometres', the Indians prefer *lakhs* (a hundred thousand) and *crores* (ten million) to the closest Western equivalents of thousands and millions, and will place a comma at the *lakh* or *crore* mark in a large number. For example, while the British would describe 50,678,954 as fifty million, six hundred and seventy-eight thousand, nine hundred and fifty four, an Indian might write 5,06,78,954 and call it five *crores*, six *lakhs*, seventy-eight thousand, nine hundred and fifty four.

Staying on the topic of arithmetic, an initial point of confusion between British and Indian English arises if an Indian says, for example, 'Four into eight'. To a Briton this might mean, 4 divided into 8 (i.e. $8 \div 4$), with the answer, 2. However, to an Indian it means 4 multiplied by 8, with the answer, 32!

For further examples from the fascinating topic of Indian vocabulary, see the table below, 'Words and Expressions used in Indian English'.

Rhyming combinations

While British English has 'mumbo-jumbo' and 'helter-skelter', similar combinations occur in Indian English, to give a gentler feel to the sentence, so instead of being told that you have come to visit for too short a time, in India you may be told that this time you came in a 'hurry-burry' and next time you should stay for several days as a guest.

Differences in accent and pronunciation

There are numerous differences in pronunciation between British and Indian English, some varying from one region to another, but one of the most universal is the difference in pronunciation of the English consonant, 'v'. Even Indians who have been educated in Christian schools and speak a version of English which most closely resembles the British one will still modify this consonant sound, giving a sound falling somewhere between British 'v' and 'w'. So the actor, Dick Van Dyke, would be referred to as Dick 'Wan' Dyke.

Another example of differing pronunciation is provided by four-syllable words, such as 'photographer' and 'economist'. Whilst a British speaker would pronounce 'photographer' in a manner resembling, 'fuh-TOG-rough-er' (stress on the second syllable), many Indians pronounce the word 'foe-tuh-GRAPH-er', stressing the third syllable. Similarly, the British pronunciation for 'economist', 'e-CON-uh-mist' becomes 'e-kuh-NOM-ist' in Indian English.

Even three-syllable words can be pronounced differently in Indian English. The British would pronounce 'generics', with a lighter stress on the first syllable, in a manner resembling, 'jun-ERIKS', while Indians give a lighter stress on the final syllable and tend to say, 'JENNAR-ix'.

The table below contains some common words and expressions that you'll come across daily during your stay in India. Undoubtedly, you'll come across several other words and forms of expressions that may surprise you.

Words and expressions used in Indian English	
Indian English	Standard English
Britisher	Briton/British
Cover	Plastic bag
Advocate	Solicitor/Lawyer
Wish ('I wish you are successful')	Hope
Doubt	Question
Hotel ('Lets go out to a hotel for dinner')	Restaurant
Pre-pone ('The meeting was pre-poned')	Bring it forward/advanced
Do this mistake ('I will always do this mistake')	Make this mistake
Like anything ('We were laughing like anything')	Very much
Indented ('Have you indented the copier paper?')	Requested
Whether you have bought gift?	Have you bought a gift?
What-all ('I need not explain what-all is happening')	Everything (concerning a subject)
Place ('We haven't enough place to work')	Space
Jug	Mug
Today afternoon (morning, evening)	This afternoon (etc.)
You do one thing	Just try this
Till date	To date
One ('Give me one bag')	A

Paining ('My finger is paining')	Hurting
What is he telling?	What is he saying?
Nothing but ('Alsatian is nothing but our familiar German Shepherd')	Clarification, which adds emphasis
I am not getting you	I don't understand what you are saying
Ragging	Bullying/Teasing
Eve-Teasing	Harassing women
Pulling ('He was just pulling me')	Making fun of ('pulling your leg')
By walk	On foot
Brown sugar	Narcotic drugs
Hot drinks	Liquor
Current	Electricity
Hostel	Halls of residence
Thanking you	Thank you
Please do the needful	Please do what is required
Dress	Clothes
Purse	Wallet
Dickie	Boot (of a vehicle)
Double confirm	Re-confirm
A Himalayan blunder	A big mistake
Godown	A warehouse
Would-be	Fiancé/fiancée
Pass out ('My son passed out from college')	To graduate

Other forms of confusing expression that you may regularly come across in Indian English include the use of a question as a statement ('Is it silver?') or the lack of proper question tags ('You like the food, no'). Sometimes an extreme statement is usually to provoke a response, especially when one knows the statement/question is untrue (e.g 'You have lost the invoices?'). Another form of expression common in the Indian corporate world is the use of the phrase 'What <your name>?' (e.g. 'What, Kris?'). This is generally used when you have actually said nothing, but the speaker uses it as a conversational opening gambit to try to throw you off balance and establish himself/herself in a dominant position.

INDIAN FESTIVALS

There is a festival or a fair celebrated every day of the year all around India. Festivals mainly celebrate religious occasions – birthdays of gods, saints and gurus (religious teachers) or advent of the year, season, harvest or the moon. A majority of festivals are common to most parts of India. However, they may be named or celebrated differently in various parts of India.

Differences of opinion about religion abound, but usually everyone is politely accommodated and religious festivals from all of the major groups can be found on the calendar. Because there are so many religious holidays, by necessity most of them only last for one day and often work continues with 'business as usual', although you may find that the post office or some other government/local government service is closed because it is a particular guru or god's birthday.

One of the longest holidays, associated with the Bengali favourite, Goddess Durga is widely known as 'Navaratri', meaning 'nine nights'. Another name for the same festival is 'Dussera', a name that emphasizes 'ten days'. Although not everyone will actually take ten days off work, it is probably second after Diwali in popularity as a festival.

The festival of Diwali (or Deepavali) is a festival of lights, with plenty of fireworks to help the celebrations (these may be much louder than the regulations permit in Western countries!). However, Diwali means different things to different people – to Sikhs it is a celebration of Guru Nanak's release from imprisonment, while to many Hindus it is a celebration of Vishnu's avatar Rama, who triumphed over the evil Ravana and returned from a 14-year exile. Diwali often falls at around the same time as the Muslim festival of Eid, marking the end of the holy fasting month of Ramadan and both festivals provide a boost of happiness as the evenings are starting to get darker.

Bright vibrant colours, illuminated religious places, brightly lit houses, plenty of sweets, traditional dress processions, dances and plenty of enthusiasm are the characteristics of all the festivals in India.

Important festivals of India

The table below shows the different festivals in India. The dates of the festivals vary according to the religious calendar.

Hindu festivals	
Baisakhi	Sankranti
Diwali	Naag Panchami
Durga Puja	Ganesh Chaturthi
Dussehra	Navratri
Onam	Pongal
Holi	Rakhi
Janmashtami	Ramnavami
Mahashivaratri	

Christian festivals	
Christmas	Easter
Good Friday	

Sikh festivals	
Guru Nanak Jayanti	Holla Mohalla
Guru Purab	Lohri

Muslim festivals	
Bakra Eid	Muhorram
Eid-ul-Fitr	

National festivals	
Children's Day	Republic Day
Gandhi Jayanti	Teacher's Day
Independence Day	

Zoroastrian festivals	
Gahambars	Jamshed Navroz

Buddhist festivals	
Buddha Purnima	

Jain festivals	
Mahavir Jayanti	

FOOD, GLORIOUS FOOD!

Food is a very important part of Indian culture. Typical Indian meals usually consist of three to four main courses, with plenty of side dishes followed by desserts. India's diversity is reflected in food as well.

Indian food (especially in southern India) may come as something of a surprise to Westerners abroad. If you are expecting a Western 'curry' (as seen in Indian restaurants abroad), then real Indian food may take some time to adjust to. While we would advise a sensible level of caution, it is an important part of the experience of India to try as many authentic Indian dishes as possible. Sometimes freshly-cooked snacks (chosen with the guidance of Indian friends) can be a safer option than dishes from apparently clean restaurants that contain pre-prepared gravies of dubious hygienic quality.

Popular and tasty snacks that you might like to try include *masala dosa* (a kind of savoury pancake with a spicy potato filling), onion *uttapam* (a thicker pancake, embedded with onion and sometimes tomato and chilli) and *poori sagu* (round and hollow, fried bread with a vegetable gravy).

Another delicious category of snacks is the *chat* items. The local favourite is *pav bhaji* (a bread bun used to mop up a satisfying chick-pea and tomato sauce). All these are vegetarian, or as they say in India, 'veg' as opposed to 'non-veg'. If you are vegetarian, or even vegan, you can manage quite nicely in India and it is a refreshing change that the term 'non-veg' makes meat-eating sound like an unusual activity.

However, this nomenclature can be somewhat misleading because in the cities of modern India (contrary to the Western stereotype of a vegetarian India), most young people either eat meat or have at least tried it. If you enjoy meat you will find that an ample number of restaurants will cater to your needs and although 'mutton' (in India this usually means goat-meat, rather than lamb) is common, expatriates in Bangalore recommend several steak restaurants where the beef is delicious.

If you are feeling conservative in your first weeks in India, Pizza Hut, Domino's and McDonald's have colonized the subcontinent. However, we strongly recommend that you try Indian dishes, especially home-cooked ones.

While many southern Indian dishes encountered in restaurants will undoubtedly appear sloppy and disappointing to the Western palate, the same meal prepared in a friend's home will be transformed into a tasty and satisfying meal.

One example which springs to mind is *sambar*, a soupy staple of southern Indian food, which is quite different from the nearest relative in northern India, *dahl* (also available in the south). The difference in taste between 'outside' and home-cooked *sambar* can be tremendous, especially when the *sambar* is mopped up with a fresh *idli* (a spongy round cake, shaped like a bar of soap, but made of fermented lentil and rice flour).

Another home-cooked treat is *chutney*, which comes in many varieties, usually bearing no resemblance to the Branston pickles and piccalillis that we regard as chutney in Britain. Homemade *chutney* is prepared by blending fried white lentils, coconut and bottle gourd (an economical Indian vegetable) and adding spices (possibly a little chilli) to taste. The result is a wonderful thick and creamy addition to any southern Indian meal, which provides a contrast in texture to the firmness of rice and the wetness of *sambar*. To indicate the wide variety of accompaniments to a meal subsumed by the word, *chutney*, you will also encounter *chutni pudi*, a powder containing broken dried red chillis, sometimes mixed with ground peanuts. This *chutney* is mixed with a little oil or clarified butter on the plate, and gives as much 'heat' as you require to a snack or meal.

Even the word 'plate' requires clarification. While many homes and restaurants will have familiar china plates, do not be surprised to find your food served on a large round metal tray with a tall rim, to prevent *dahl* or *sambar* from spilling. At cafés, plates may be cheap plastic, wiped only with a dirty cloth (caution!) while surprisingly one of the cleanest plates you will find is a fresh banana-leaf, thrown away after the meal is finished.

Like other countries, India has its junk food, with omelettes, veg-fried rice/noodles and 'cup-noodle', which is similar to the British 'pot-noodle'. However, the undisputed champion of junk food is probably *gobi-Manchuri*, which translates as 'Manchurian cauliflower'. It is my understanding that the name is just a gimmick and it is probably unknown in the northeast of China. The dish can roughly be described as cauliflower combined with onions, garlic and spices, fried in a batter that is rich in red or orange food colouring. While *gobi-Manchuri* is probably not healthy to eat every day, it is undoubtedly a tasty change when you are bored with eating your usual canteen food, and it tends to be safe and satisfying, especially with a freshly cooked Indian flatbread (*roti*, *naan* or *chapatti*).

Sweets are extremely popular all over India and are usually cooked in a lot of fat and sugar. Indian sweets are not usually eaten to finish off a meal, as they are in Britain, but are more commonly bought for a celebration (this can be anything from a family occasion, a house-visit, a graduation or birthday, to the most trivial excuse!). The variety of sweets is breathtaking and there is something for every taste at dedicated sweet shops. However, nearly all of these contain milk, and if you have a sensitive stomach it may be necessary to be cautious, restricting yourself to sweets from a good shop with a rapid turnover.

Eating out

Eating out is a regular event in India that you are likely to enjoy just as much whether you are out with friends on a shopping trip, going for a 'treat' to celebrate a friend's birthday, or simply having a cheap meal after work when you are too tired to cook. The majority of the restaurants in India are open from 6 am to 10 pm.

Chats

Indian eateries come in all shapes and sizes, and at the simplest level you can visit outside *chat* stalls in which the snacks (*chats*) are freshly prepared before your eyes. The food is cheap and satisfying, with popular items like *bhel puri* (a snack prepared from puffed rice, chopped onion, small pieces of potato and coriander), topped off with optional sweet and spicy sauces, *pani puri* (crispy fried hollow spheres of wheat with a spicy wet sauce), *masala puri* (similar, but with accompanying spicy chick peas, rather than sauce) or *pav bhaji* (split bread bun 'puffs', lightly toasted on one side to mop up a delicious vegetarian stew made from tomatoes, cauliflower, potato, greens and spices).

It is said that Indian ladies cannot go shopping without visiting a favourite *chat* stall or cart, and once you sample the range of snacks available, you will understand why!

Indian fast food eateries

At a slightly higher level of eating is one of the semi-outdoor cafés or *hotels* (this term is used for a restaurant in India) in which customers eat fast food at small tables or counters that have no chairs and you just stand and eat. The food is inexpensive, fresh and hot and in southern India you can choose from a variety of *dosas* (savoury pancakes), *idlis* (rice and white-lentil patties) or *vadas* (savoury fried mini-'doughnuts'), each accompanied by a spicy *sambar* (lentil gravy) and coconut *chutney*.

In the north of India you can get scrumptiously satisfying *chapattis* (flat bread) or parathas (crispy part-fried flat breads that may be plain or have a filling such as potato or cauliflower). These breads may be accompanied by delicious chutneys that tantalize the tastebuds, or *cholay/channa masala* (a protein-rich spicy chick pea dish). Especially at breakfast you may encounter *puris* (also spelt 'pooris'), which are deep-fried and soft (rather than the hard-fried *puris* that come with *chats*) and made from wheat-flour. Alternatively, for Sunday lunch, you can meet the *puri's* big brother, the *bhatura* (made from plain flour), together with *channa masala*, spicy pullao and a dash of pickle for a meal that will leave you fit to burst.

In these small, fast food eateries, especially in southern India where thin gravies (*sambars*) or pepper water (*rasam*) are ubiquitous, the food comes on either a compartmentalized metal tray (*thali*) or a flat circular stainless steel dish with a tall rim so that your gravy can't spill, but can easily be mopped up with rice or bread (OK, or a spoon if you aren't ready to go fully native!).

The cheapest lunch available at basic indoor *hotels* is the so-called *meals*, that consist of a plate (which may actually be a banana leaf) of small vegetable dishes, pickles, *dahl* or *sambar* (lentils) and rice, that is refillable, meaning that young waiters will keep spooning more onto your plate until you are incapable of swallowing another mouthful! If you are served food on a banana leaf, the correct etiquette is to sprinkle water on it (to clean off dust) before eating and then smooth the water off the leaf. Finally, fold the leaf lengthwise towards you to indicate that you have finished your meal.

Local restaurants

The next level of restaurant is the kind that you might go to for a reasonably-priced evening meal, where you sit down upstairs in a clean restaurant with table cloths and waiter service. Most of the dishes we have already discussed (except *chats*) will be available, as will soups, vegetable fried rice, *romali roti* (a large thin bread, cooked on a steel hemisphere and folded like a handkerchief), and a wide variety of vegetable dishes (e.g. *aloo capsicum*, made from potato and green pepper). Additionally (if it is not a pure 'veg' *hotel*), meat dishes like 'butter chicken' or 'chicken 65' will come up on the menu (although beef and pork are taboo).

In coastal regions you may find that more coconut oil is used in cooking, or fish dishes are available (fish is a passion in West Bengal!). Wherever you are, you will be sure to come across the so-called 'Manchurian' dishes, like *gobi Manchuri* (spicy cauliflower fried in a red batter), and *baby corn Manchuri* (similar, but made with sweet corn as a popular starter). Often the smaller *Manchuri* vegetable items are flavoured with finely chopped garlic and come with cocktail sticks so a group of friends can easily share a platter while waiting for the main course.

High-level restaurants

Above this level of restaurant (which is perfectly satisfactory), you will find venues where the cost of your meal may approach that of a medium-priced dinner in Europe, but where the standard of service and interior décor is exemplary and may be nicer than any restaurant you have eaten at before. The food is also impressive, with not just all the usual dishes, but also chef's specials, unusual starters like *hara bara kebab* (a colourful green vegetarian starter), and *continental* (meaning European or American) foods and Chinese dishes.

In fact, Chinese food is available in almost all 'sit-down' restaurants in India, but it may not be quite what you are used to. While the spicy 'veg. fried noodles' are now practically as Indian as rice and curry, other noodle dishes in India may be less flavoursome than you are used to, while curiosities like spicy veg. fried rice and dishes with vegetables in a sauce are still described as 'Chinese' when they are really at least 60% Indian. Like Chinese and Indian food in the UK, Chinese dishes in India have clearly been adapted to the host nation's tastes.

Chinese food has been popular in India for a long time, and for many years each big city has had at least one or two *continental* restaurants. However, as an inevitable consequence of globalization, Pizza Hut, Domino, KFC and McDonald's (or variations thereof) are also spreading like wildfire. More vegetarian alternatives are available in these franchises (and sometimes assurances that any meat is *halal*), and the menu may be a little different from the one in your home country, but if you feel like you need a reminder of home, it is available.

In the last few years, even Mexican and Thai cuisine has become available. The stereotypes are being broken and now Indian eating is really going global, so it is no wonder that India's restaurants are always busy, providing the perfect mix of tasty food, a pleasant atmosphere and good value for money.

These and many other pleasurable experiences await you in the world of Indian cuisine, to which we can only add, *bon appetit* and watch your waistline!

Northern Indian food

Food name	Type
Chapati	Thin Indian bread made out of wheat flour
Dum gosht	Lamb curry
Tandoori chicken	Chicken roasted in tandoor (clay oven)
Biryani	Spicy rice mixed with spices vegetables or meats
Naan	Thick Indian bread made out of wheat flour
Paratha	Wheat flour bread with vegetable stuffing inside
Roti	Wheat flour
Chole	Chick peas curry
Korma	Mild curry made with cream and vegetables
Dal	Type of lentil
Bhatura	Bread made of wheat flour and fried
Rajma	Curry made of red kidney beans

Southern Indian food

Food name	Type
Dosa	A pancake made of ground rice
Idli	A steamed rice cake
Upma	Semolina snack
Sambar	Stew made of lentils and vegetables
Rasam	A light soup made of tomatoes
Bonda	Dumpling made of vegetables and flour
Bajji	Vegetable fritters
Vada	Spicy doughnuts
Uttapam	A rice pancake with a topping of onions, tomatoes and chillis
Payasam	Rice dessert
Appam	Ground rice pancake
Idiappam	Steamed rice noodles
Chicken 65	A deep fried chicken spiced with onion and ginger
Pongal	Rice cooked with black pepper

Western and Eastern Indian food	
Food name	Type
Pav	Bread
Dahi vada	Fried spicy doughnuts dipped in yoghurt sauce
Puri	Fried bread
Bombil fry	Fried fish
Vindaloo	A spice curry made of chilli paste
Veg Kolhapuri	Vegetarian dish cooked in tomato sauce
Dhokla	Gram lentil cake
Upmaa	Semolina
Chakli	A grain flour savoury snack
Bhaji	Vegetable dish
Dhansak	Lentil curry
Kichidi	Rice cooked with lentils
Aludram	Potato curry
Tel Koi	Bengal fish curry

INDIAN SPICES

There is probably no other country that uses as many kinds of spices as India. Spices are cheap and plentiful. However, they are commonly referred to with local names.

Here's a list of spices commonly used in Indian cuisine and their English equivalent.

Name	Type
Aadrak	Ginger
Badam	Almonds
Dalchini	Cinnamon
Dhania	Coriander seed
Elaichi	Cardamom
Haldi	Turmeric

Hing	Asafoetida
Imli	Tamarind
Gur	Jaggery (unrefined sugar)
Jaiphal	Nutmeg
Jeera	Cumin
Kala Mirch	Black pepper
Kesar	Saffron
Khus Khus	Poppy seeds
Lavang	Cloves
Mehti	Fenugreek
Mirch	Chilli
Namak	Salt
Pudina	Mint
Rai	Mustard
Til	Sesame

INDIAN SWEETS

Food name	Type
Gulab Jamun	Fried flour balls served dipped in sugar syrup
Jalebi	Fried flour and yoghurt coated with sugar syrup
Kulfi	Milk ice cream
Peda	Milk sweet
Rasgulla	Curdled milk balls dipped in sugar syrup
Ras Malai	Indian cheese dipped in sweet milk
Halwa	Paste made of flour, almonds and ghee
Coconut Burfi	Grated coconut mixed with syrup
Kesari Bath	Semolina based sweet
Payasam	Pudding
Puran Poli	Sweet bread made of milk, gram and jaggery

4
Immigration

INDIAN IMMIGRATION SYSTEM

Unlike Western countries, India does not have an integrated immigration policy. Indian immigration regulations are quite complex and often frustrating, without any proper structure. India has only recently experienced an influx of businesspeople and foreign nationals relocating there. A visit to an Indian mission abroad will give you a glimpse of how frustrating the regulations will be.

Whilst Indian missions abroad (Division of the Ministry of External Affairs) issue visas, immigration matters in India are handled by the Bureau of Immigration, the Ministry of Home Affairs and the local police. Superintendents of the Police have wide powers on immigration matters in India.

There is no provision of 'visa on arrival' in India. All foreign nationals except Nepalese, and Bhutanese citizens require a visa to travel to India. However, citizens of Nepal require a visa when entering India from China. Nationals of the Maldives do not require a visa for entry into India for tourism purposes only and can stay up to 90 days. Foreigners carrying a valid PIO (Person of Indian Origin) Card or OCI (Overseas Citizen of India) Card along with their valid national passport are permitted to enter India without obtaining an Indian visa separately. Please note that

Train at remote hill station in India

Munnar, tourist destination in South India

Narmada River meandering through a narrow gorge at Jabalpur

Typical Indian marketplace

Sunset in Bangalore

Farm on outskirts of Mysore city

Water taxi in Kashmir

Residential area in the new city of Chandigarh

Autorickshaw on the streets of Bangalore

© 2007 ooyoo/iStock

Dusk in Mumbai

© 2007 Zsolt Langviser/iStock

Mountain top monastery in the Indian Himalayas

Victoria memorial, Kolkata

Women in traditional saris in front of the Taj Mahal

Western railway headquarters, Churchgate, south Mumbai

Shore Temple, Mahabalipuram

separate visa regulations exist for diplomatic/official passport holders.

Even before your trip to India begins, the first hurdle is to obtain a visa. The forms are available online from the Indian Missions abroad (for example, see www.hcilondon.net/visa/entry-visa.html) and the process appears straightforward, but it is not. On a busy day Indian embassies and consulates have the atmosphere of a bustling Indian market, with plenty of pushing, shoving and shouting. It certainly pays to enter with plenty of patience and good humour. If you have not visited India before, then a trip to the Indian mission to apply for a visa may be your first real contact with Indian culture.

As such it is quite an experience and may give you your first inkling that the 'real India' is not quite what you had imagined from television programmes replete with *sitar* music, or a 'curry' with your mates on Friday night!

WHERE TO APPLY FOR INDIAN VISAS

You'll need to apply for an Indian visa at the Indian Embassy, High Commission or consulate in your country of residence, well in advance. Most Indian missions issue the visa on the same day if applied for in person. The first surprise is just how many people want a visa to visit India – you may well find yourself queuing for an hour outside the Indian mission even if you have arrived early in the morning. Be prepared to wait inside the Indian mission for the whole day.

There are no standard application forms and you'll need to fill in a visa application form issued by the respective Indian mission abroad. The structure of the form even varies within each country. Please ensure that you have filled in the correct form designated for that particular embassy or consulate, as Indian missions have been known to refuse application forms issued by other Indian missions within the same country (for example, in Australia, the Indian Consulate in Sydney will not accept visa applications with forms issued by the Indian High Commission in Canberra). Visa fees will have to be paid in cash. Currently, the cost of the visa varies according to the applicant's nationality and type of visa issued (see table below). The visa fee also varies from country to country.

Visa application forms and guidance notes can be downloaded from the Indian mission websites. A full list of Indian missions abroad is available at meaindia.nic.in/onmouse/mission.htm.

You'll need to have your passport valid for a minimum of six months beyond the date of intended departure from India. The following types of visas are available from Indian missions abroad.

Major types of Indian visa	
Tourist visa	Usually given for six months with multiple entries. You'll need to submit the application along with a return air ticket and show proof of financial support. Tourist visas are non-extendable in India.
Business visa	Usually given for one year or more with multiple entries. You'll need to submit the application along with a letter/fax from the sponsoring organization indicating the nature of business, duration of stay in India, places, organizations to be visited and a guarantee to meet your financial expenses.
Student visa	Usually issued for the duration of the academic course of study or for a period of five years, whichever is less. You'll need to submit the application along with a letter of admission issued by the educational institution in India. In some cases where a further referral is required from authorities in India, student visas can take up to two weeks to process. Please note that the student visa will not permit you to change the status of the visa or the educational institution. A fresh application will have to be made to the FRO (Foreigners Registration Office, see below) if you wish to change academic institution in India.
Transit visa	Usually issued for a maximum period of 15 days with single/double entry facilities to transit passengers only. You'll need to submit the application along with a return air ticket and show proof of financial support.

Journalist visa	Issued for media professionals visiting India for work. You'll need to submit the application along with a letter/fax from the sponsoring organization indicating the nature of business, duration of stay in India, places, organizations to be visited and a guarantee to meet your financial expenses. You are also required to contact on arrival in New Delhi, the External Publicity Division of the Ministry of External Affairs and in other places, the Office of the Government of India's Press Information Bureau. Journalist visas usually take at least 12 weeks to process.
Employment visa	Also known as 'E' visas are issued to professionals or persons who are appointed by companies or organizations in India. You'll need to submit, along with your application, proof of contract/employment by the company or organization in India. The duration of visa varies according to the contract of employment. Please note that the employment visa will not permit you to change your employment status (change of company). A fresh application will have to be made to the Indian mission abroad in your country of residence or at FRRO/FRO (Foreigners Regional Registration Office/Foreigners Registration Office, see below) if you wish to change your employment status in India. Students and graduates who are going to India to do an internship/work experience programme with an Indian firm are required to apply for an employment visa.
Other visas	Other types of visas are issued by Indian missions abroad. These include dependant/spouse visas, missionary/religious visas, conference, academic research visa and visas for medical visits.

Different categories of visas with specific restrictions or endorsement of numbers of entries allowed and duration of stay in India are mentioned on the visa.

Transfer of visas

Visas issued on old/expired passports can be transferred to new passports by Indian missions abroad for a nominal fee. You'll need to fill in a new application form.

Wrong type of visa or stamp

Your visa is valid from the date of issue. If you realize or feel that you have been issued with wrong documentation, then contact the Indian mission/office of issue immediately. It is best to check your documents and visa upon issue as the wrong type of stamp can cause a bureaucratic nightmare in India.

ARRIVING IN INDIA

As soon as you arrive in India you'll have to go through immigration. Unlike other countries, India does not have a separate arrivals queue for its nationals. You'll need to complete a disembarkation card on which you'll be asked your full name, sex, date of birth, nationality, passport and visa details, address in India, occupation, flight number, date of arrival/boarding and final destination in India. The Immigration Officer will then validate your arrival with a stamp on your passport. The bottom half of the disembarkation card is also stamped and attached to your passport. This will be retained by the Indian customs whilst you go through the customs check. The Indian Bureau of Immigration has telephone contacts for general enquiries at major ports of entry.

Contact details for Bureau of Immigration
Delhi Airport: 011-25652389
Mumbai Airport: 022-26828098
Kolkata Airport: 033-25208100
Chennai Airport: 044-23454977
Amritsar Airport: 0183-2592986

DOCUMENTS TO CARRY WHILE GOING TO INDIA

Immigration Officers at the port of entry rarely request any supporting documents for your purpose of stay/visit to India. However, it is advisable to carry copies of your employment contract, business letters, documents from educational institutions or other supporting documents. Customs officers have been known to request the documents whilst inspecting bags.

POLICE REGISTRATION IN INDIA

Now that you have arrived in India, you'll have to go thorough a few more bureaucratic formalities. If you are residing in India on a visa allowing more than a six-month stay (i.e. not a tourist visa) then you are legally required to register at a local police station within your first two weeks in India. A reminder to do this should actually be stamped on your visa, but don't forget. Police registration, within 14 days of arrival in India, is required for all foreign nationals (including Persons of Indian Origin) above the age of 16 staying in India (on any type of visa) for more than 180 days in a single visit. A separate provision exists for Pakistani and Afghan nationals. Pakistani nationals are required to register in India within 24 hours of arrival, whilst Afghan nationals are required to register within seven days of arrival in India. Children below the age of 16 do not require registration on any type of visa.

This requirement applies to those on a student visa (including those coming for study of yoga, vedic culture, Indian system of dance and music), research visa, employment visa, missionary/religious visa and visas for medical purposes irrespective of the duration of their stay. Holders of business visas are exempt from the registration requirement if the duration of their stay does not exceed 180 days on a single visit. If circumstances change and you are planning to stay for more than 180 days on a business visa then you are required to register your stay before the expiry of 180 days.

WHERE TO REGISTER

Police registration facilities are not provided at the airport, but are carried out in designated Foreign Regional Registration Offices (FRRO) located in the five major cities of India (see table below) or at the District Superintendent of Police who also act as the Foreign Registration Officer (FRO).

Complete information regarding Indian immigration rules, including the addresses and telephone numbers for the FRRO offices, police registration and visa extension forms can be found at the Bureau of Immigration website at www.immigrationindia.nic.in.

Foreign Regional Registration Offices in India	
FRRO Delhi	East Block-VIII, Level-II, Sector-1, R.K. Puram, New Delhi-110066 Tel: 011-26711443, 26195530, Fax: 26171944 Email: frrodli@nic.in
FRRO Mumbai	3rd Floor, Special Branch Bldg., Badruddin Tayabji Lane, Behind St. Xavier's College, Mumbai-400001 Tel: 022-22621169, Fax: 022-22620721 Email: frromum@nic.in
FRRO Kolkata	237, Acharya Jagdish Chandra Bose Road, Kolkata-700020 Tel: 033-22470549, Fax: 033-22470549 Email: frrokol@nic.in
FRRO Chennai	Shastri Bhawan, 26, Haddows Road, Chennai-600006 Tel: 044-23454970, Fax: 044-23454971 Email: frrochn@nic.in
FRRO Amritsar	123-D, Ranjit Avenue, Amritsar-143001 Tel: 0183-2508250 Email: frroasr@nic.in

In all other major cities foreigner registration is carried out by the District Superintendent of Police who acts as Foreign Registration Officer. As mentioned earlier, Superintendents of the Police have wide powers on immigration matters in India. They can grant a temporary extension of stay subject to further clearance from the Ministry of Home Affairs, New Delhi.

REGISTRATION PROCESS

To a large extent, the police are a law unto themselves and it is best to be very polite, respectful and appreciative. While India has an anti-corruption bureau and Indians are required to swear oaths against bribery, some police officials (more likely the ones who have desk jobs as clerks) may ask you to grease their palms. This suggestion may come in the form of, 'I have helped you very much, haven't I? You should give me some gift'. Sometimes they may feel a little ashamed (or afraid of being caught) and if you ask how much, you may be told, 'Just friendly … friendly'. It is best to take your company's representative or a friend who speaks the local language and will know how much *bakhsheesh* (bribe/tip) is required.

Nowadays bribes (which are not always asked for) should not be too high. Also, remember not to use the word 'bribe' or bring up the subject. If the Indian police require anything, they will find a way of letting you know. In one case (while getting a visa extension) we remember being asked to walk outside the police station, take a folded piece of paper, place some money inside and bring it back to the counter. When a 100 rupee note was not enough, a second trip outside and a total bribe of 200 rupees saved the day.

It is important that you go for Police Registration accompanied by an Indian (most likely from your company's Human Resources department) who speaks the local language. We noted this in the southern Indian city of Bangalore where we observed that the police representative who dealt with foreign nationals could not speak a word of English.

DOCUMENTS REQUIRED

Although the requirements change every few years, at present it is best to bring along with the completed application form:

1. Your passport and photocopies of the main page.

2. Photocopies of your Indian visa.

3. Your offer letter from the company and a signed 'joining letter' (which in a company is likely to be your contract).

4. A letter from your company certifying that you are an employee, at what date you joined, in what capacity and if the contract is not an ongoing one, the duration of your employment.

5. Proof of your Indian address (which may be a copy of your rental agreement). This may be a little difficult within the first two weeks of your stay in India, because you may be in a company guest house for the first few weeks until you can find longer-term accommodation in an apartment. However, your company can provide an equivalent letter if you do not yet have a landlord (or your landlord is unprepared to give a rental agreement for tax reasons).

6. Six passport-sized photos (all of which must be identical).

7. It may also be helpful to bring a company ID card and possibly some business cards, but this is not actually required.

8. Your company medical report might also be worth bringing, although the requirement of a mandatory HIV test for foreigners has thankfully been dropped.

You should take three or four copies of each of items 1 to 5.

The registration is free and usually takes a few days to process. An initial visit to the police station will clarify the current requirements before a second trip to finish the registration. You will be lucky if you can complete this process within a couple of visits to the registration office, and it may be that you have to sit down and wait for long periods in the police station. Sometimes you may be asked to come back the next day for no apparent reason, but you must be patient, good-natured and polite throughout. Occasionally your accompanying local friend may have to be firm about the help you need, but you should not. Be over-respectful to the police and they will treat you well.

You'll then be issued with a certificate of registration (Part III of Form A) by the registration officer. You'll need to keep this document in your passport at all times whilst in India, as you may be asked to produce this document within 24 hours by the local police, magistrate or tax officer. You'll also be asked to surrender this document when you are leaving India by the Immigration Officer at the port of exit. It is advisable to make several copies of this, along with your passport as it will assist you in case you lose/destroy the original document.

RESIDENCE PERMIT

The first step of your dealings with the police is now over and you will have a stamped certificate from the FRRO/FRO. However, you'll need to get the PAN (Personal Account Number) card. This is required (so the police say) because many foreigners have been coming to India, avoiding tax, then leaving before the tax year is over and depriving the Indian goverment of enormous sums of money. Whatever the truth of this, you need a PAN card in order to get a residence permit, which is what you require from the police to legally live and work in India.

For further details on PAN please refer to the Chapter 6.

Finally, a short and painless trip to a previously designated FRRO/FRPO/police station to which you should take both your Police Registration Certificate and the PAN card will give you your Residence Permit.

CHANGE OF DETAILS/LOST REGISTRATION

You'll also need to update the FRRO/FRO with any change of your status or address in India. For a lost registration document, you'll have to make a fresh application in writing for a duplicate copy providing the details of the loss of the certificate and your passport.

LOST PASSPORT AND EXIT PERMIT

It gets slightly more complicated for loss of passport. You'll need to make an application in writing to the nearest FRRO/FRO and submit it along with a copy of the police report, a letter from your embassy with details of the lost passport and the new passport/travel document details. The FRRO/FRO will then issue you with an exit permit after making a few enquiries.

LATE REGISTRATION

By law you are required to register within 14 days of arrival in India. Late application usually complicates the matter and gets referred to senior police officers who'll then request further documents and reasons for late submissions in writing. There is also a penalty fee of US$30 payable in equivalent Indian currency.

EXTENDING YOUR VISA IN INDIA

Tourist visas cannot be extended or changed to other visas in India, and a fresh application will have to be made at an Indian mission abroad. Other visas, can usually be extended up to a year. The extension application will have to be submitted to the nearest FRRO/FRO along with supporting documents. You'll need to submit in writing the reason for extension and include supporting documents from your company, businesses, educational institution or other organizations. If it is your first extension then, the FRRO/FRO usually grant an immediate three month extension and refer the case for consideration by the Ministry of Home Affairs (MHA), New Delhi. Upon approval by the MHA, the FRRO/FRO will then grant a further nine month extension. Subsequent extensions, on a yearly basis for further four more years can be granted by FRROs/FROs (except in the case of citizens of China and Sri Lanka).

BRINGING IN YOUR DEPENDANTS

You can bring your spouse, children and family members to India while you are working. They are permitted to stay with you for the duration of your employment in India. It is advisable to apply for a dependant visa at the Indian mission abroad. This will enable your spouse/dependant to extend or change the status of their visa should they decide to work or stay on further. The Officer at the Indian Mission abroad will want to see copies of your passport/Indian visa and your employment contract and will generally grant an (X-Other) entry type of visa. Unmarried partners are not granted dependant 'X' visas and may only be granted a Tourist visa. The validity of this visa will depend on the validity of your employment visa. After arriving in India, your spouse/dependant should register with the police and obtain residence permits. Your spouse and dependants can seek further extension on their visa as you extend your employment/business visa. Dependants are not automatically permitted to work in India. A fresh application will have to be made at FRRO/FROs for a change of visa status.

OVERSTAYING OF VISA

Another bureaucratic nightmare. It is advisable to approach the FRRO/FRO well before the visa expires for a temporary extension. The Immigration Officer at the port of exit will not permit you to leave the country on an expired visa. FRROs/FROs can regularize overstay up to three months beyond the validity of your original visa (excluding tourist/transit visa) in the case of reasonable grounds of delay. However, an overstay penalty fee of US$30 plus a visa extension fee of US$40 is charged in equivalent Indian currency. In all other cases matters will have to be referred to the Ministry of Home Affairs, New Delhi. You'll need to make a fresh application in writing, stating the reason for overstaying and submit it along with your passport and pay the required fee. The FRRO/FRO will then grant an extension for you to leave the country or refer the matter to Ministry of Home Affairs, New Delhi.

RESTRICTED/PROTECTED AREA PERMITS

A Restricted/Protected Area Permit is required by all foreign nationals to travel to the following regions within India:

- the whole of State of Manipur;
- the whole of State of Mizoram;
- the whole of State of Arunachal Pradesh;
- the whole of State of Nagaland;
- the whole of State of Sikkim;
- parts of the State of Uttaranchal;
- parts of the State of Jammu and Kashmir;
- parts of the State of Rajasthan;
- parts of the State of Himachal Pradesh;
- the Whole of Union Territory of Andaman and Nicobar Islands;
- parts of the state of Sikkim.

The permit is free and is issued by the Resident Commissioner of the state concerned, FRRO/FROs of the state/region concerned or by Ministry of Home Affairs, Foreign Division, Jaisalmer House, 26, Man Singh Road, New Delhi. You'll have to make an application in writing stating your purpose of visit and duration of stay in the region. The permits are issued on the same day.

CUSTOMS REGULATIONS

Custom regulations change quite frequently (almost every year) and vary according to your port of origin. You are advised to check with the Indian Customs website at www.cbec.gov.in before travelling. Generally you are prohibited to bring any of the following into India: drugs, explosives, firearms, Indian currency (except in the case of passengers normally resident in India who are returning from a short visit abroad, where they are permitted to import Indian currency up to Rs5000), pornographic material, counterfeit and pirated goods and antiquities.

Indian Customs also have a special provision for people residing abroad and transferring residence to India for a minimum period of one year; this is the 'Concessions for Transfer of Residence' which allows you to bring in more household goods than normal without paying duty. If you are importing or exporting goods, a licence or Customs Clearance Permit (CCP) and Import Export Code number has to be obtained.

Trafficking in narcotic drugs is a serious offence under Indian law and is usually punished with long-term rigorous imprisonment.

CONTACTING YOUR EMBASSY FOR HELP

Most countries have diplomatic representation in India. You may have to register with your embassy depending on your national requirements. It is always useful to have the contact details of your embassy in case of any trouble. The contact details of a few diplomatic representations in India are shown in Appendix 2. The majority of the countries have consulates in Mumbai, Kolkata and Chennai and honorary consulates in other cities. For more details check with your embassy website. A full embassy listing is available at www.meaindia.nic.in.

5
Travel

TRAVEL TO INDIA

The quickest way to India is by air. Major airports in India with good international and domestic connections are Mumbai, Delhi, Kolkata and Chennai. Other major airports in India with direct international flights to London, Paris, Frankfurt, Bangkok, Singapore and the Middle East are Bangalore, Amritsar, Trivandrum, Ahmedabad and Hyderabad.

Indian airports serving international airlines
Delhi Air India, Ariana, Air France, Air China, Austrian, Aeroflot, Alitalia, Austrian Airlines, Biman, British Airways, Cathay Pacific, Delta Airlines, Druk Air, Gulf Air, Ethiopian, Emirates, Etihad, Indian Airlines, Jet Airways, Kenya Airways, Korean, KLM, Oman Air, Northwest, PIA, Qantas, Qatar Airways, Royal Nepal, Royal Jordanian, Saudi Arabian, Swiss, Singapore, SAS, South African, Srilankan, Virgin Atlantic, Thai, Turkish Airlines, Turkmesnistan Airlines and Uzbekisthan Airways
Mumbai Air India, Air France, Air China, Austrian, Aeroflot, Alitalia, Austrian Airlines, Biman, British Airways, Delta Airlines, Cathay Pacific, Gulf Air, Ethiopian, Emirates, Etihad, Indian Airlines, Jet Airways, Kenya Airways, Korean, KLM, Lufthansa, Oman Air, Northwest, PIA, Qantas, Qatar Airways, Royal Nepal, Royal Jordanian, Saudi Arabian, Swiss, Singapore, SAS, South African, Srilankan, Virgin Atlantic, Thai and Turkish Airlines

Kolkata Air India, Biman, British Airways, Cathay Pacific, Druk Air, Gulf Air, Emirates, Etihad, Indian Airlines, Jet Airways, Lufthansa, Royal Nepal, Royal Brunei and Singapore Airlines
Chennai Air India, British Airways, Cathay Pacific, Gulf Air, Emirates, Etihad, Indian Airlines, Jet Airways, Lufthansa, Oman Air, Qatar Airways, Saudi Arabian, Singapore, Srilankan and Thai
Bangalore Air India, British Airways, Gulf Air, Emirates, Indian Airlines, Jet Airways, KLM, Lufthansa, Oman Air, Qatar Airways, Singapore, Srilankan and Thai
Hyderabad Air India, British Airways, Gulf Air, Emirates, Indian Airlines, Jet Airways, KLM, Lufthansa, Malaydian, Oman Air, Qatar Airways, Singapore, Srilankan, Saudi Arabian and Thai
Trivandrum Air India, British Airways, Gulf Air, Emirates, Etihad, Indian Airlines, Jet Airways, Oman Air, Qatar Airways, Singapore, Srilankan and Saudi Arabian
Ahmedabad Air India, British Airways, Gulf Air, Emirates, Indian Airlines, Jet Airways, Oman Air, Qatar Airways, Srilankan and Thai
Amritsar Air India, British Airways, Gulf Air, Emirates, Indian Airlines, Jet Airways, Turkmesnistan Airlines and Uzbekisthan Airways

Telephone numbers of major international airports in India	
Amritsar: +91-183-2592166	Goa: +91-832-540806
Ahmedabad: +91-79-286 9211	Bangalore: +91-80-5277944
New Delhi: +91-11-25652021	Chennai: +91-44-2560289
Mumbai: +91-22-26156600	Kolkata: +91-33-25119977
Hyderabad: +91-40-27903785	Thiruvananathapuram: +91-471-500283

GETTING AROUND IN INDIA

One of the most important factors affecting your stay in India will undoubtedly be the Indian transport system, a multi-headed beast which, if tamed, can be a valuable ally during your stay.

If you are in India for a short visit, then you'll probably use escorted taxis with no difficulty, but you will inevitably need to negotiate India's roads to get around town. Roads and especially rail and air travel, are required for the long distances between Indian cities.

DRIVING

In India, like the UK, Japan and Australia, vehicles are driven on the left-hand side of the road and visitors and new residents should have a valid international driving licence. You are permitted to drive on an international driving permit for up to a year in India.

Driving licence

To get an Indian licence you'll need to apply at the Regional Transport Office (RTO) of the city/town you live in. The process is quite simple if you go through an agent (usually a driving school). It is advisable to apply for a licence through a driving school as they will handle all paper work for a small fee. They will give you driving lessons that you may need to overcome the 'initial fear' of driving on Indian roads.

Along with the application, you'll need to submit the photocopy of your residence permit (see Chapter 4), proof of your age, proof of your address (utility bill or a letter from your employer) and four passport-sized photographs. The fee for an Indian licence varies from state to state. You'll initially be issued with a learner's permit and then, after three months, the full licence. Your Indian licence will be valid until your residence permit expires.

Driving around towns and cities is not recommended. Indian roads are a nightmare. The majority of the drivers are reckless, impatient and dangerous drivers. Parking is also a major problem in big cities and towns. Be aware that, if you drive yourself, there could be a risk of involvement in a long nightmare with the Indian police and possibly a lengthy court case if you have an accident.

You are better off hiring a local driver and a car on contract with a rental agency. There are several in every town and city. Your Indian colleagues will recommend one. The local drivers know the region well and are used to the roads and driving conditions. It is best to look for an experienced, older driver rather than a young, reckless driver (many young Indian drivers are!). It may even be cheaper to find a driver with his own car.

Renting a car

Although you'll see many private car rental companies all around the city, you'll find it is almost impossible to rent a car without a driver in India. It is also safer to rent a car with a professional driver who is used to the driving conditions. Most of the foreign embassies recommend hiring of cars with drivers rather than the car itself. Car rental, inclusive of driver, is inexpensive by Western standards.

Buying a car

India has the world's second largest car market. Brand new cars are priced from 400,000 rupees, while good second-hand cars are available from 100,000 rupees. A good place to look if you are planning to buy a second-hand car is in the classified section of the major Sunday newspapers. Also www.motors.ebay.in, www.bharathautomobiles.com and www.carsalesindia.com have good listings of second-hand cars for sale. Unfortunately, there is no standard booklet (issued by the government) that advises on what to look for when buying a second-hand car. To get an idea of what you should be paying it is best to ask your Indian colleagues or friends. Also get an independent mechanic to test the car before buying. Look around at as many cars as possible before buying.

By law, your car must be registered, taxed, insured and pass the pollution test. Registration and road tax can be applied for at the Regional Transport Office (RTO) of the town or city you live in. Again, if you wish to avoid the paperwork involved in the registration of your vehicle, then it is advisable to approach a driving school which will handle the process for a small fee. Vehicle insurance is available from a wide number of insurance companies. Your Regional Transport Office (RTO) or the driving school will have a list of local insurance company offices and their agents.

Motorbikes and bicycles

Best not to bike around the towns and cities as serious bike accidents resulting in head injuries are frequent (almost daily) in India. Roads are heavily congested. Besides, most of the motorists in India do not respect cyclists and often harass them on the road. Brand new motorbikes are priced from around 40,000 rupees for an Indian-made two stroke 100 cc engine bike to up to 200,000 rupees for imported bikes. Second-hand motorbikes and scooters are available from 10,000 rupees.

PUBLIC TRANSPORT

Modern Indian companies and branches of MNCs (Multi-National Companies) are often located on the outskirts of Indian cities and are sprawling farther and farther afield as the cities expand. Along with the expanding educated workforce, this means that highways to the city limits are now amongst the most congested roads you will encounter.

Local or company buses

You may earn enough to employ a driver, but if not or if you want to save some money, you may have to depend on the company bus. These buses are often better than normal public buses, having better suspension, but may not go as far as to have air-conditioning like some of the interstate buses. The best way to keep cool is to open the window a little (careful of the dust!) or draw the curtain a fraction if the glare of the sun is uncomfortable. Company buses pick up workers at designated points, and may either wait for half an hour for the employees to board, or arrive at a designated time to pick up the workers. In either case IST ('Indian Slow Time') is followed and the bus may come late, occasionally early, or sometimes not at all. If you have to wait for your bus in the heat of the sun, a hat is advisable.

In general, the usual protocol of women sitting at the front and men at the back of the bus is followed on company buses, as it is on public transport, but all the passengers use the same door at the front of the bus. This differs from sardine can-packed public buses, in which ladies, the elderly and the handicapped use the front door while able-bodied young men use the rear door! The segregation on buses is mainly to prevent Indian men from misbehaving with women, and even if you are travelling on the local bus with a female Indian friend who is guiding you, the bus conductor will remind you to get to the back of the bus in no uncertain terms.

Travelling on public local buses alone is generally to be avoided. While they are very cheap, public buses may not go to where you want, necessitating a more circuitous route than by a taxi or autorickshaw. More importantly, they are so tightly packed that it is hard to get off at your stop and it can be impossible to avoid being pick-pocketed.

Commuter trains

Suburban trains exist only in big cities (Mumbai, Delhi, Chennai and Kolkata). However, they do not serve all parts of the city. They are cheap and, like public buses, they are always crowded and not clean. First class is usually available. Commuter trains offer the option of buying tickets weekly, monthly or yearly (travel cards/pass). Tickets are not sold on board and you'll have to purchase a ticket before you board the train.

Taxis/autorickshaws

For day-to-day travel around towns and cities, and especially if you miss your bus to work in the morning, taxis and auto-rickshaws (*auto*) are very useful. In India both taxis and autorickshaws can be recognized by their distinct colour (usually yellow and black). Usually four people can travel in a taxi or three in an auto.

By law both taxis and autorickshaws must have a standard meter inside, and fares are set by the local government. Auto and taxi fares are very reasonable. Insist on the driver using the meter unless you know what the fare should be, in which case you can negotiate accordingly. However, it may be that taxi or auto drivers are reluctant to travel to certain areas of the city if it is hard to find a fare for the journey back, and then they will ask for a large gratuity for their trouble.

Sometimes the auto driver may ask 'service' or 'direct'? Service autos operate in some, but not all cities and are designed to carry seven people, rather than the usual three (in reality, a service auto can squeeze in up to 15 people!). When a conventional auto illegally stretches the normal complement of three passengers to four, they will usually ask for a 'one and a half' fare. However, the service auto charges only a nominal fee, following a fixed route and will pack the passengers in to increase the driver's earnings, with ladies sitting on one seat, facing men on the other, if both must share a sevice auto. If the driver of a conventional auto rickshaw offers you the option of 'service', rather than 'direct', remember that although the price will be far lower, he will stop many times to pick up passengers and if you are hoping to reach a place on time, you may be disappointed. Dedicated service autos are not available in every city, but are very common in Hyderabad, where they resemble a stretched version of Mr Bean's Reliant Robin!

Auto rickshaws tend to chug out lungfulls of fumes, but in most cities they are now meant to use LPG (Liquefied Petroleum Gas) as a fuel instead of petrol, which is much cleaner-burning. This is slowly making an impact on the quality, if not the quantity of traffic pollution in India's cities.

The base charge on the meter in an autorickshaw may vary slightly from one city to another, but currently is around 10–15 rupees. However, in some of the costlier cities, auto drivers may become a little cheeky and refuse to drive anywhere for less than 20 rupees. Even worse, they may refuse to use the meter (insist on 'meter' or find another driver) or be very selective about which routes they will travel – so much so that as a joke, Indians usually say to an auto driver, 'Okay, where do you want to go?'.

In most cities if you see an autorickshaw, or especially several autorickshaws together at the side of the road, it is generally best to avoid asking these drivers. They are usually lazy and will refuse to drive to your destination, or quote an exorbitant fare. Instead, it is better to flag down an empty autorickshaw driving past. The drivers will often slow down if they see a foreigner, expecting that you may need a lift. As a rule of thumb, auto drivers who are looking for a fare tend to kerb-crawl more slowly at the side of the road, while full autos speed past in the mainstream of the traffic. You can summon a passing autorickshaw by shouting 'Auto!', which is pronounced a little like 'Otto!'. Sometimes this is accompanied by a hand-waggling gesture, particularly when ladies are beckoning a cab.

Very occasionally, the taxi or auto driver will over-readily and smilingly agree to take you 'by meter', knowing he has cranked the meter to go round twice as fast as normal! Another trick that a foreigner might come across is an over-friendly driver who offers to take you anywhere in the city for the ridiculously low price of 10 rupees. Of course, there is a catch, namely that along his route he will stop for 'just five minutes' to take you to a government handicrafts emporium which has offered him a deal. There they will give you a free soft drink and try to convince you to buy Indian souvenirs – carvings, carpets, sculptures, jewellery, all at marked prices. They will tell you there is no obligation, but will try every trick in the book to pressurize you into buying and then look very sad and disappointed when the 'rich foreigner' leaves empty-handed!

Of course, whenever you are in an unfamiliar city and travelling by meter, you must be careful that the driver does not take you on a tour of the city when your journey should take just 15 minutes. If it looks like this is the case, tell the driver to stop immediately, or say, 'police-station!'. There is often a number written on the back of the driver's seat, with instructions to phone if he tries to cheat you.

Some cities are distinctly different, like Chennai (Madras) in which the autorickshaws and taxis do not use meters at all and it is imperative that you agree to your journey's cost in advance. In Kolkata (Calcutta), taxi-cabs are a more common means of transport than autos, but you still have to take the same precautions with the fares.

Interstate buses

The interstate buses are cheap, convenient and comfortable. They are often air conditioned and are not packed like public buses. These are run by private coach companies or the government run SRTCs (State Road Transport Corporations). For example, in Bangalore or Mysore, you would book a KSRTC (Karnataka State Road Transport Corporation) bus, while in Hyderabad, it would be an APSRTC bus (Andhra Pradesh State Road Transport Corporation) showing the respective states in which the city you start your journey from lies. They can be booked online, but this can be a difficult rigmarole and it may be easier to reserve your seat at one of the numerous booking cabins dotted around your city. It may not be possible for a friend to book your ticket, even online from a different state and you also may need the help of someone who knows your regional language if you book from a small cabin. The bus times are highly variable and depending on traffic conditions, your bus may be an hour or more late, its departure may not be announced, and there may be no clear identification as to where it is going.

Having said that, the interstate coaches are quite reasonably priced, and while you may not get a proper night's sleep you can recline the seat and the driver will generally stop at designated stops for refreshments or even by a roadside bush if you are desperate for the toilet! With interstate buses, the ladies front/gents back rules do not apply because tickets are merely assigned in order of booking time, with first come, first served. However, even on interstate buses the driver or his assistant may politely ask you to exchange seats if it can prevent a woman having to sit next to a man!

Rail travel

Ever since colonial times, India has had an extensive rail network which generally functions pretty well. Indian trains are very economical and relatively comfortable, provided you travel in sleeper class or above. A complete list of its extensive network and schedule is available online at www.indianrail.gov.in.

You should book your travel in advance to avoid the unbooked 'cattle-truck' class (sometimes you can book a train just two or three days in advance, but it may be better to book a week to ten days before travelling). Advance booking is especially important when it is a festival or the school holidays, so check if you are going to risk booking just a few days before your journey. Local Indians recommend that foreigners should pay a little more and travel in the more comfortable, air-conditioned coach. However, we have always found that sleeper class (in which you have either an upper or lower basic, but comfortable bunk-bed type sleeping arrangement) is perfectly adequate.

Indian rail journeys can be booked at a railway station (which involves queuing or in some cases, pushing!), designated railway booking centres around towns and cities, via a travel agent (your company may have one), or simply online. While booking at a train station do look for a separate designated queue for overseas visitors. These queues tend to move a lot quicker. You'll have to fill in a 'bookings form' (available at train stations), where you'll need to mention the destination, passengers' names, ages and your full Indian address before you proceed to the counter. You may be asked to present your passport if you are booking the tickets under the foreigner visitor quota.

The quickest and the easiest way to book is online. The booking can be made at www.irctc.co.in in which 'IRCTC' curiously stands for 'Indian Railway Catering and Tourism Corporation limited'. The website requires registration in which (strangely!) you have to match your Indian cheque or bank book to your username online. After a little effort registering on the website (which sometimes freezes or times-out half way through your booking) you can simply print out your own ticket. When you reach your train, your name will be printed on a sheet near the door of your train carriage (indicated in the ticket or at the station notice board). As a foreigner, you are also entitled to book under the tourist quota: Indian Railways sets aside a few seats on each trip for overseas visitors and during peak season it may be easier to find a seat under the tourist quota.

When you book your train journey, there is a choice of upper, middle or lower berth, or upper or lower side berth. The lower berth doubles up as a seat wide enough for three passengers during the day time and then when the traveller in the middle berth is ready to turn in for the night, the middle bunk is hooked up. The top bunk is fixed, so you can lie down at any time if you have booked it (and your feet have plenty of room to poke out if you are tall). However, if you want to maintain a close watch on your shoes and luggage (there are plenty of stories of shoes being stolen), then you are a little far from the floor. If you have just a small item of light luggage and you can sleep comfortably, it may be best to keep it with you up on the top bunk if this is the one you have booked. These three berths are arranged at 90° to the length of the train. However, there are also side-berths that are parallel to the length of the train and are a little shorter than the normal bunks. Also, your feet cannot stretch out beyond the length of the bunk, so usually these seats will be the last ones to be booked. Surprisingly, although men and women are segregated in buses, on trains men and women may be sleeping on neighbouring bunks.

The Indian train journey really is a fantastic way to see India, looking through the bars of the train window (except in the air-conditioned carriages) and seeing every temple, paddy field, village, factory and small station along the way. You will hear tea and coffee-vendors going up and down the train singing, '*kaffeee-kaffeee! Chaiii, chaii, garam-garam chai!*' ('coffee, coffee, tea, tea, hot-hot tea!'). Also orders for soft drinks, snacks and dinner will be taken by train staff. The meals are surprisingly good and, in our experience, hygienic too. In India the accepted procedure for disposing of your paper plate or plastic tray after the meal is to throw it out of the window!

Along the journey there are stops at small stations where you can get steaming hot food. This may mean freshly cooked *idlis* and coconut *chutney* wrapped in a banana leaf if you are in southern India, or if you are in northern India it may be some kind of vegetable fried in a spicy batter (*bhaji/pakora*). Packets of potato crisps and carton drinks, lollipops and ice-creams are also available and vendors will come onto the train, as well as the occasional beggar, asking for '*rupee/paise*'.

Railway service telephone numbers	
General: 131	Arrivals: 133
Reservations: 132	

Safety on trains

You are cautioned to politely refuse any food offered to you by fellow passengers, in case it is drugged and you wake up with a missing wallet (or, according to urban myths, kidney!). Also ensure that your luggage is secure as there have been reports of thefts on the trains.

An Indian train journey in unbooked 'cattle' class is certainly a sensory experience, and most Indian railways carry the distinctive smell of '*eau de lavatoire*'. One of the oddest parts of the journey if travelling in an unbooked class or sleeper class is that you will encounter the *hejiras*, described by Indians as 'eunuchs', although that is not really what they are. In the West we might refer to them as transsexuals dressed in sarees and one or two of them will walk up and down the train begging for money, perhaps offering to sing for money. Generally they will pinch men's cheeks and generally try to harass them until they cough up some money. Usually the best thing to do is ignore them, and then the worst thing they can do is gently put their hand on your head and spit out of the window (which is taken as a *hejira* curse).

The journey on any Indian train will be memorable, as well as the views out of the open train door at the end of each carriage where you can watch the countryside flashing by. All in all, while the train may sometimes only be an hour faster (occasionally even an hour slower) than an interstate bus, it is far more comfortable and is an important part of the Indian experience. In the early morning as you pull into little stations, or even your final destination, the relaxing 'bing-bong' sound of the station tannoy lets you know you are enjoying the unique experience of the Indian railways.

Air travel

The quickest way to travel around India is by air. The possibility of flying between Indian cities is, of course, the preferred mode of transport if you can afford it, and in some cases the flight costs (booked online in advance) can compete with the railway tickets. You arrive feeling fresh, without the exhaustion of a long bus or rail journey and with far more time to spare for your trip. However, you may find (depending on your time of arrival and the city you are visiting) that while your flight may be just one hour, the taxi journey from the airport to the hotel or company you are visiting may take two to three hours if you hit the rush hour!

Airlines in India have a policy of charging all foreigners US dollar tourist fare (usually 25% extra). To get the standard Indian rupee fare you'll need to mention to the airline or the travel agent that you are resident in India while booking. You may be required to present a photocopy of your residence permit (see Chater 4) at the airport.

India, like UK and Europe, has jumped feet first into the low-cost airline boom, with several airlines vying for the routes between India's major cities. The main players are currently Jet Airways, Indian Airlines, Air India, JetLite, IndiGo and Kingfisher. The standard of service on board these airlines is extremely good with plenty of food (even on short flights) and refreshments.

Air Deccan and SpiceJet are no frills airlines offering extremely low fares between major Indian cities. However, they are frequently late and do not keep passengers well informed. SpiceJet recently broke into profit, a feat which the other low-cost airlines in India have not yet accomplished.

Flights can be booked directly on the airline's website or at any travel agent in India.

Airlines operating flights within India
Indian Airlines: 1800 180 1407; www.indian-airlines.nic.in
Air India: 1800 22 77 22; www.airindia.com
Jet Airways: 1800 22 55 22; www.jetairways.com
JetLite: 1800 22 30 20; www.jetlite.com
Kingfisher: 1800 2333 131; www.flykingfisher.com
IndiGo: 1800 180 38 38; www.goindigo.in
SpiceJet: 1800 180 33 33; www.spicejet.com
Air Deccan: 1800 425 7008; www.airdeccan.net

TRAVEL AGENCIES

There are plenty of independent travel agencies offering competitive air fares in major towns and cities. Travel agencies in India also specialize in booking bus and train tickets, hiring cars with a driver and arranging short 'sight seeing' trips to nearby places of interest.

Online travel agencies offering similar facilities in India include:

- www.ezeego1.co.in;
- www.travelguru.com;
- www.makemytrip.com.

6
Employment in India

The profusion of jobs in India and growing globalization means more and more foreigners work in India. The traditional Indian work environment has some remnants of the British Raj: detailed rules and responsibilities, and strict protocol while conducting business. But modern, multinational companies tend to create a similar environment all over the world.

Many foreigners may find it positive that English is the principal language of business in India. In some of the companies, especially IT companies and call-centres, working far beyond office hours is not just hinted at but made obligatory. In more traditional companies, people work strictly within designated office times, mostly 9:30 am – 5:30 pm. The idea of a Saturday holiday is gaining ground but not adopted everywhere.

RECRUITMENT

Most recruiting in India is still fairly informal: walk-in application and interviews are common for jobs below the managerial level. In speciality areas like finance, engineering and marketing, on-campus recruitment is often used to find graduates. Recruitment through the web and recruitment agencies is now growing in India. You are advised not to look for a job in India on a tourist visa.

EMPLOYERS

As an expatriate you can apply directly to the company you wish to work for. Companies have a list of vacancies on their websites. Indian companies have started advertising in career sections of European newspapers. The majority of Indian companies have also started actively seeking graduates from abroad.

Indian IT firms have started to attend careers fairs at universities in Europe and in the US. You can compile a list of companies in India that you are interested in working for from newspapers and magazines and then contact their human resource departments.

NEWSPAPERS

Newspapers are another excellent source of jobs in India. The majority of Indian newspapers carry extensive lists of jobs in India. Indian newspapers that are useful to look into include:

- *The Times of India* (www.indiatimes.com);
- *The Economic Times* (www.indiatimes.com);
- *The Hindu* (www.hinduonnet.com);
- *Indian Express* (www.indianexpress.com);
- *Asian Age* (www.asianage.com);
- *Hindustan Times* (www.hindustantimes.com);
- *The Deccan Herald* (www.deccanherald.com).

INTERNET SITES

Internet job sites like Monsterindia.com, Yahoo (in.jobs.yahoo.com), jobsahead.com, timesjob.com and Naukri.com are becoming popular. These websites have Indian job sections where you can post your resumé online. You can click on a recruitment consultant's website and talk to a senior manager about your interest in working in India over the phone.

APPLYING FOR A JOB

When you apply for a job at an Indian company, don't be surprised if you don't get an immediate response – this may be your first experience of Indian flexible punctuality (a phenomenon referred to in India as I.S.T., or Indian Standard Time!) and is perfectly normal.

Your first contact with an Indian employer may come in the form of a telephone interview with your future boss, followed by a chat with a human resources representative. The telephone interview can be a little tricky, especially when you are talking across cultures and both you and your prospective employer don't know quite what to expect. However, there is no need to worry, just treat the interview as a friendly chat.

While you may have heard that you should negotiate hard and not be cheated, don't worry about this on the initial contact. Remember that it is often a bonus for an Indian company to recruit employees from overseas, especially from the West. Your interviewer may well be an Indian who has worked abroad (the USA is a common destination) so he/she could be pitching the interview in an American style, or from a stereotypical image of how a corporate interview in the West should take place. Jokes meant to lighten the atmosphere may misfire and expressions may not cross cultures, but remember that however it may sound, the Indian company is going to a lot of trouble to recruit you and it is not in their interest to intentionally cause any offence.

Your interview may include obvious questions, such as why you want to work in India (be prepared to answer this repeatedly when you arrive in India!) and what your career plan for the future might be. There will also probably be a pitch about the strengths of the company.

The interview will be followed up by e-mail contact and possibly a meeting with an HR representative, if the company is big enough to have international offices. Before you meet a company representative, make sure that travel expenses will be reimbursed as this may not be standard practice for the company. Indian HR representatives abroad are likely to be the company's best, and they are not only likely to be polite but also will give you an impressive presentation convincing you that they can match the standards of any Western company (take this with a pinch of salt). The HR representative may also explain to you that the company has strict salary gradation points, and there is no possibility of salary negotiation (don't believe this!).

Application forms

Curiously, it may be only after these contacts and meetings that the company gets round to e-mailing you their application form! When you do receive the form, you may notice significant differences between an Indian application form and one from your home country. Information which might be considered personal or confidential in the West may well be requested, such as the salaries of your family members and your family's total income! Do not worry; as a foreigner you should not have to fill in such details and you can leave them blank.

It may take a month or two for Human Resources to respond and provide you with a letter confirming your appointment and organise your flight. Don't worry, this is perfectly normal and does not mean they have lost interest in you. Your HR or recruitment contact in India may finally mail you, saying that they haven't heard from you for some time (even though you sent them the application form weeks ago and have had no response!). The HR department may just be stalling and trying to excuse themselves, but you must also remember that in India if you don't keep hassling someone, it is often interpreted to mean that you are actually not that bothered!

THE INTERVIEW

When asked to join an interviewing panel in India, we were a little surprised when the first question posed to an Indian job applicant concerned her family background – including her parents' and brother's professions! Ostensibly, the explanation for this is that a complete picture of the candidate's background will help employers determine whether the applicant will be comfortable within the company. However, it might also be fair to say that a natural curiosity about someone's family and social background pervades Indian society – even in professional circles – and that concepts of privacy and data protection are not yet as deep-rooted as they are in the West.

Apart from the telephone interview and the meeting with a human resources representative, you may also be invited to an on-site face-to-face interview in India, if the position you are applying for is a senior one.

When offered a position, it is best to negotiate monthly allowances for housing, relocation expenses, etc. and have these as part of the contract.

WORK PERMITS OR RESTRICTIONS

Indian immigration law does not require a work permit. A company has to sponsor you to come to India for work. The most important document is the contract of employment with the Indian company which will state the duration of employment, the salary and other benefits.

Unlike Western countries, the Indian government has not placed any restrictions on foreign nationals working in India. Employment visas are also required for spouses or dependants intending to start and run their own businesses in India (see Chapter 4).

WORK ENVIRONMENT

The working environment in India has many things in common with the Western workplace, sporting a high level of technical acumen amongst its workers and a relative ease of communication in English. However, you may come across a number of differences which require explanation.

One thing that you will soon notice is that just as Indian society is hierarchical, so is the Indian workplace. In general, Indian society respects seniority, and especially in the Indian academic world people are expected to 'respect their seniors' and 'juniors' may often be treated like servants. 'Ragging', or academic bullying of new students still occurs to some extent. These attitudes may still be in evidence in the corporate environment, but an employee's level (and especially salary) in the company may supplant traditional hierarchical systems.

Regional affiliations and nepotism may also exert an influence. Do not be surprised to hear stories of bosses favouring people from their own state in India, or that the CEO's friend or relative has been awarded an important contract.

Low-level workers

However, these aspects of the system are less important than the stratification that you will come across on a day-to-day basis. Indian companies are adopting very modern professional systems, but some features of a traditional, hierarchical structure are difficult to shake off when cheap labour is readily available. This means that even in a major company you can find very low-paid workers assigned to act as tea-boys, errand boys, rubbish collectors and floor-sweepers. Needless to say, these employees may speak only a basic level of English, if any. However, they are very useful and you will probably spend more time interacting with them than with high-level bosses.

Second level

The second level in your company's hierarchy is the workers with an intermediate level of qualification (which may be as high as a Master's degree). These workers are really the backbone of the company and are young, highly competent people who may be worked very hard by the tiers above them in the company. This second tier usually speak good English and are better-paid than the first tier, but are often still underpaid, especially when they have a family to support. For this reason, people in the second level of the company switch jobs very frequently for the '40% hike' in salary expected when hired by a new firm. While there may be a variety of job titles such as 'junior manager' and 'assistant manager' with graded rises in salary, the reality is that the second-level workers have many years of hard graft ahead of them, often with little opportunity for promotion.

Third level

The third level is perhaps what we would term 'middle management' and may occasionally contain some determined second-level workers who have risen up through the ranks to deputy-manager level. However, the preferred worker in this category is one having acquired qualifications or experience overseas ('foreign', especially 'Western' credentials carry a lot of weight, with experience in the USA trumping that from other countries). Middle managers earn a relatively comfortable salary by Indian standards, and at the highest level this may even compare with a low-level salary in a Western country.

Fourth level

At the fourth level, the managers, who are assisted by several deputy-managers must typically deal with even larger amounts of bureaucracy than middle-managers. At the same time, the deputy-managers must use their experience to keep challenging projects on track and interview employees: a demanding task in today's India, where workers shift jobs on a regular basis. Managers get a good salary, commensurate with the administrative duties and pressure they are subjected to from their own superiors.

Hierarchy

You may feel that nothing you have heard so far is really different from what you have experienced in a Western company. However, in India there is a significant difference in the way that the various levels of the company communicate. Indian workers at different levels in a company are not treated as equals and superiors may verbally harangue their inferiors in a way that seems completely unacceptable to a Westerner. Although this may make you feel uncomfortable, the air of superiority displayed by bosses is required to maintain a social distance and prevents junior employees from taking advantage of them. If you treat junior employees as equals in the way you would in the West, they may soon start testing the limits and attempting to take advantage. This may involve an office boy asking you your salary, telling you how low his is and then asking for money. Alternatively, it may involve juniors doing favours for you in order to obligate you to 'help' them. This help may range from asking for money to obtaining favours in terms of promotion or a putative job in the UK or USA that juniors may believe you can 'get' for them.

So do not be surprised when you first join an Indian company to have junior employees pulling up chairs for you, ordering their inferiors to bring you cups of tea or bringing snacks for you. This may be innocent Indian politeness towards a foreigner or a higher-ranking employee, but if it persists such behaviour may well be intended to obligate you. This obligation may become explicit if you resign from the job and find the over-friendly office boy who insisted on bringing you tea and snacks expecting you to give him your television or other items from your flat in recognition of his efforts!

Formality and informality

In India, there is more deference to authority and reluctance to call people by their first names. But there is also genuine informality in dealing with people and wary Westerners may find what is called their 'personal space' invaded.

Women colleagues may get some unwelcome attention. Wearing T-shirts for daily work is not acceptable except in some IT industries. Some of the attitudes may seem less professional, but there is a simplicity in behavior which can be refreshing.

A further difference is in communication in terms of the level of verbal 'directness' used in the Indian workplace. This often means that Indians will speak in a way which a Westerner would regard as 'ordering people around' or 'being bossy'. However, in India this is regarded as quite normal 'professional' behaviour and even a friend might say, 'You do one thing …', before making a suggestion, rather than, 'You could try …', that might be used in the West (see Indian English in Chapter 3).

Another difficulty that you may come across is obfuscation. If an employee has not carried out a task or has arrived late for work, then he may find no end of excuses and sometimes will talk around in circles, repeating your question back at you in the hope that you will become bored and give up. There are times when you must be firm, but do not lose your temper as there may have been a genuine misunderstanding, so it is important not to jump to conclusions.

EMPLOYMENT CONTRACT

The general hiring practice in India is for employers to provide the recruit with a letter of appointment that also serves as a contract. This letter will include your position, responsibility, start date, salary, allowance, transfer, company rules and a clause for termination of employment.

SALARIES

Wages in India are quoted in *lakhs* (sometimes spelt, 'lacs'), i.e. 100's of thousands. When you have converted your salary into Western currency (see conversion chart in Chapter 2) you will appreciate that a generous Indian salary is still relatively modest by Western standards. However, the cost of living is also moderate by American or European standards.

Furthermore, to understand your take-home salary, it also helps to understand a little about the Indian tax system.

General salaries in India vary sharply by academic qualification and work experience. At the entry level a call-centre operator or IT programmer may earn as little as 100,000 rupees (around $2,500) annually, while a software engineer with reasonable experience will earn about 500,000 rupees (about $12,000). Middle management wages in some IT sectors are on par with the West. Salaries are currently increasing at a rate of 10–20% annually in India. Average salaries in India for various professions can be found at www.payscale.com/research/IN/All_People_in_All_Surveys/Salary.

Your wages in India will also be compensated by certain 'perks'. Income compensation in India is paid through fringe benefits, flexible benefits and retirement benefit. This type of compensation is usually around 40–65% of your gross salary. Besides this, you'll also be offered performance-based pay and other allowances.

This system was developed due to the rising cost of living for Indians and to enable the companies to utilize tax exemption status under Indian taxation laws. However, with the introduction of fringe benefit tax (FBT) in 2005 these benefits are being reduced, but they still remain as an important part of Indian corporate pay structure.

The flexible benefit plan (FBP) is another standard corporate practice in India where an employee is allocated a certain value in benefit. The employee can choose how to utilize the benefit. Such benefits can include rent, mortgage payments, transportation, purchase of white goods, health expenses, education and low interest loans.

EMPLOYEE BENEFITS

General employee benefits in the Indian corporate sector are very competitive. The majority of companies benefits include:

- highly subsidized food;
- free life, travel, health and disability insurance;
- company-paid training;
- yearly rewards and service recognition.

Besides this, companies also offer paid maternity leave for female employees, payment towards provident fund (social security), paid holidays and stock options.

EQUAL OPPORTUNITY

India does not have an equal opportunity act and government jobs are reservation based (in terms of caste and religion). However, the Indian

Equal Remuneration Act 1976 prohibits discrimination between men and women either in the matter of recruitment or payment of wages when the jobs are identical, except when the employment of women in certain types of work is prohibited or restricted by law.

TAXES IN INDIA

Generally speaking the company you are working for will deal with all your income tax contributions. However, to understand your take-home salary, it helps to understand a little about the Indian tax system.

Firstly it must be remembered that for an annual salary up to 110,000 rupees, there is no tax. While you are unlikely to have a job with such a low salary, it means that the first 110,000 rupees (145,000 for women and 195,000 for people aged 65 years and above) of your annual salary is exempt from tax.

Tax rates (2007–8) are:

- 10% between 110,001 and 150,000 rupees;
- 20% between 150,001 and 250,000 rupees;
- 30% plus 4,000 rupees (5,000 for women) between 250,001 and 1,000,000 rupees (your salary will almost certainly fall into this category).

For salaries above 1,000,001 the tax is still 30% but there is a surcharge of 10% of the total tax liability.

All taxes in India are subject to an education charge of 3% of the total tax payable.

The company you work for is likely to mitigate this tax to some extent by stipulating that certain components of your monthly wage are benefits, which are taxable at a lower rate.

Furthermore, Indian residents can avoid up to 30% of the tax by investing in schemes endorsed by the government, with companies such as Reliance Industries, ICICI bank, or other major companies. To do this it is necessary to submit a company tax return at the beginning of the tax year (March), or at least before the end of July, declaring the intention of investing at least 80,000 rupees.

However, these investments which are in the region of 80–100,000 rupees must be kept for at least 3 to 5 years. This means that if, for example, you earn around Rs50,000 per month, you will have to invest around two months' salary to avoid losing one month's salary in tax. It still may be worth making such an investment, because even if you only work for one or two years, you can still get your investment back after the three-year lock-in is over.

Because of the difficulties of trying to retrieve the investment from abroad, accountants usually advise expatriates that it is hardly worthwhile investing if the stay in India is for only one or two years. Their reasoning is that for a modest saving there are many international phone calls and possibly even a return flight to India, and then money might be lost on bank charges transferring investments back to the West. Most of these factors could probably be circumvented with care and the help of the right contacts, but a short-term investment may still be an unnecessary headache. You may end up paying full tax until your investment is declared, but the subsequent tax should be deducted (with a reduction, if necessary, in later months to compensate for earlier months with full tax) so that over the whole financial year you are not overcharged.

Certain tax relief, incentives, rebates and allowances are also available to foreign nationals in some sectors (specialist knowledge, invitation by the Indian government, academic programmes, etc.). These are listed at www.incometaxindia.gov.in.

INCOME TAX PERMANENT ACCOUNT NUMBER

Everyone employed in India needs a PAN (Personal Account Number) card, which is roughly equivalent to a social security number in the UK or the US. A Permanent Account Number is a ten-digit alphanumeric number, issued by the Income Tax Department. A typical PAN would be VVA1S1205E. It is compulsory for companies to quote a PAN on payment of income. You'll also need a PAN card in order to get a residence permit. It is also required by foreigners engaging in business financial transactions in India and for making deposits exceeding Rs50,000 at a bank or post office.

Applying for Income Tax Permanent Account Number

To get the PAN card quickly (ten days to two weeks), it may be best to pay a visit to your company's accountant (or one whose services they contract), who should be able to provide the necessary forms and process them without charging you anything. You can also apply online or in person at designated IT PAN Service Centres in India. There is a processing fee of Rs60 plus tax for all applications made in India.

Online PAN application

It is best to apply for a PAN online as applications made via the internet are treated as a priority and you'll receive your PAN by email within a couple of days. Application for a PAN can be made online at www.tin-nsdl.com. However, you will still need to print the application, sign it and submit it at designated IT PAN Services Centres in your city along with required proof of identity, proof of address and a passport-sized photo. You will be informed of your new PAN by email a week after receipt of application. The PAN card will be posted to your residential address.

Applying in person

You can apply for a PAN in person at any of the designated IT PAN Services Centres in your city which are managed by UTI Investor Services Ltd (UTIISL). You can locate the nearest one in your city online at www.utiisl.co.in, www.incometaxindia.gov.in or www.tin.nsdl.com.

You'll need to fill in the required form (Form 49A) and submit the required proof of identity, proof of address and a passport-sized photo. Your passport with an Indian visa is sufficient for proof of identity. The following documents are accepted as proof of address:

- copy of electricity or telephone bill;
- bank or credit card statements;
- letter from the employer;
- Indian driving licence;
- certificate of address signed by a Member of Parliament, Member of Legislative Assembly, a local Councillor or a Gazetted Officer (notary).

You'll receive your PAN card by post within a month. You can track the status of your application online at https://tin.tin.nsdl.com/pan/index.html or by phone at 0124-2438000 (or 95124-2438000).

WORKING HOURS

The standard working week in India under the Factories Act is usually 48 hours for adult workers. Working hours in offices are generally between 35 to 40 hours. Hours worked in excess of the standard hours are generally paid at overtime rates. However, in certain sectors (IT, call centres, medical, etc.) you may be required to work unsociable hours or beyond office hours. These would normally be stated in your contract.

PAID HOLIDAYS AND TIME OFF

There are between 15 and 20 paid public holidays in a year. This depends on the state you live in. Provisions will also be made for paid time off and time off for medical reasons. These again will be stated in your contract of employment.

WORK EXPERIENCE, INTERNSHIPS AND VOLUNTEER PROGRAMMES

An increasing number of Indian companies have started offering work experience and internships to students and graduates overseas.

Surprisingly, a majority of Indian companies offer paid internship and also pay costs of your travel from your home country. Most companies also offer direct employment after a period as an intern. However, you are advised to apply well in advance as places are limited. The 'In-Step,' internship programme launched by Infosys Technologies had about 8,500 applications for 100 available internships in 2005.

Application process

Applications are best made directly to the human resources department of the company where you wish to do your internship. You can apply online for most of the companies. The internship generally ranges from two to six months. If your initial application is successful, then the company will contact you for a telephone interview.

A number of web-based private internship/placement companies have sprung up recently offering internship programmes in India. Most of them claim to offer fully paid internships for a small fee. You are advised to be cautious while dealing with these companies.

The benefits

A majority of companies offer a student/internship stipend during the entire internship duration. This allowance varies between 10,000 to 40,000 rupees. Most of the companies also offer accommodation during your internship.

Internship visa requirement

As a prospective intern in an Indian company you'll need to apply for an employment (E category) Visa and **not** a student visa. For further details on the application process please refer to Chapter 4.

Volunteer programmes

Opportunities for a number of volunteer programmes exist in India. They include social work, conservation work, teaching opportunities, health care, etc. To visit India as a volunteer you'll need to apply directly to the voluntary organization you are interested in. Most of them accept online applications.

A list of voluntary organizations that operate in India is given below.

List of voluntary organizations operating in India
Volunteer in India: www.volunteeringinindia.org
Overseas Working Holiday: www.owh.com.au
Global Volunteer Network: www.volunteer.org.nz/india
Volunteer Work Abroad: www.volunteerabroad.com/India.cfm
Indian Volunteers for Community Service: www.ivcs.org.uk
Global Cross Road: www.globalcrossroads.orfg
Oxfam: www.oxfam.org.uk
Voluntary Service Overseas: www.vso.org.uk

Volunteer visa requirement

As an unpaid volunteer in India you'll need to apply for a tourist visa and **not** an employment visa. For further details on the application process please refer to Chapter 4.

7
Business in India

Business-wise, India is opening up and international companies are investing in India. European and American companies which were hesitant to do business with India in the 80s and 90s are now opening subsidiaries in India. Today India is Asia's fourth largest economy and has had an average growth rate of eight per cent during the last three years. The economy beat expectations and grew at a rate of 9.2% in the third quarter of 2006. Manufacturing recorded a growth of 2.9% in 2006, services including real estate and communication grew at a rate of 13.9%. Imports for the year 2006-07 grew by 21.59% and exports by 20.9%. The Indian economy has gained momentum with high investment and consumption demand.

India also benefits from being the world's largest democracy and has had a fiercely independent judiciary based on British law. With a market of over one billion people, a large middle class and 55% of the population below the age of 25, India has become an ideal business destination. However, India is still trying to overcome the red tape of its early 'licence raj' system which you need to be aware of.

RED TAPE

According to the World Bank, India is still one of the most difficult places in the world to start a business. It can take up to two months on average to set up a business in India compared to a few days in Europe. It is difficult to set a business up by yourself. Many of you will not be used to the ridiculous amount of paperwork required, long queues (in Mumbai, people queue all day to get their papers stamped) and dealing with government officials. Dealing with bureaucracy or any government departments in India takes time. You'll need plenty of patience. It is best to have a local consultancy firm or an Indian partner to guide you through the early registration process.

Further details on setting up a business in India can be found at:

- www.india.gov.in;
- www.indiainbusiness.nic.in.

CONSULTANCY COMPANIES

A number of private consultancy companies have recently been established (both in India and overseas) to assist in setting up businesses in India. They provide a range of services including:

- full legal services regarding doing business in India;
- incorporating a company in India;
- opening a branch office;
- opening a project office;
- setting up joint ventures in India;
- setting up a subsidiary in India;
- drafting agreements;
- negotiating agreements;
- setting up outsourcing in India;
- dispute resolution.

A full list of these companies and their services provided is available online at:

- www.amchamindia.com;

- www.assocham.org;
- www.ciionline.org;
- www.ficci.com.

TYPES OF BUSINESS ENTITIES

The choice of entity depends on your circumstance. You may wish to set up a sole proprietorship or go into partnership with your Indian colleagues.

The following types of business entities are available in India:

- private limited company;
- public limited company;
- unlimited company;
- partnership;
- sole proprietorship.

Besides incorporation in India there are other ways of establishing a business in India and these are as a branch office of a foreign company, a liaison office/representative office or a project office.

For the registration process you'll need a corporate lawyer or a chartered accountant to register the name of your company in India. The process involves the usual filling in of numerous forms, paying a small fee and suggesting at least three names for the company/business. It takes around a week for the Registrar of Companies to inform you whether the proposed names are available. After you decide on the name, your lawyer will then prepare an article of association and file it with the Registrar of Companies along with the fees. The fee currently varies with the value of share capital.

Generally, prior approval is required from the Reserve Bank of India before investing in India. Some categories of businesses are covered under an automatic approval process and these are listed at www.indiainbusiness.nic.in.

There are some minor post-incorporation filing formalities, after the remittance of capital from overseas to India that need to be completed. You'll also need to look into the following:

- obtaining a Permanent Account Number (PAN) (See Chapter 6);

- complying with the Shop and Establishments Act;

- registration for import/export code from the Director General of Foreign Trade;

- Software Technologies Parks of India (STPI) registration (if necessary).

TAXES IN INDIA

The Indian tax structure is well-developed with clear demarcation of authority between central and state governments and local councils. Central government levies taxes on income (except tax on agricultural income) customs duties, central excise and service tax. State governments levy taxes on sales, professions and on proceeds from land revenue. Local authorities levy taxes on properties, water supply and drainage, entertainment tax, etc.

Value Added Tax (VAT)

Although Value Added Tax replaced sales tax in 2005, it has not been fully implemented by all states in India. State sales tax is still applied in some states. At present VAT is applied at 12.5%.

Corporate Income Tax

Income is taxed at a flat rate of 30% for Indian companies, with a ten per cent surcharge applied on the tax paid by companies with a gross turnover over ten million rupees (one *crore*). Foreign companies pay 40% tax. As with income tax, an education charge of three per cent (on both the tax and the surcharge) is applied, yielding effective tax rates of 33.99% for domestic companies and 41.2% for foreign companies. From 2006 the filing of tax returns became compulsory. All companies incorporated in India are considered as domestic Indian companies for tax purposes, even if owned by foreign companies.

Fringe benefit tax

Fringe benefits are charged at 33.99% of the benefit seen by the employees. This is only a percentage of the actual amount paid.

Tax benefits

The government of India provides several tax incentives to promote employment and new investments.

These are subject to specified conditions, and are available for:

- infrastructure;
- power distribution;
- some telecom services;
- starting industrial parks or special economic zones;
- production or refining of mineral oil;
- business involved in research and development;
- developing housing projects;
- operating in certain rural hill states;
- processing of food grains;
- food processing;
- rural hospitals, etc.

Several other incentives are offered to export businesses or industries located in Export Processing Zones (EPZ).

Tax incentives for export

The new export–import policy provides substantial tax incentives for investments in Export Oriented Units (EOU) and industries located in the Export Processing Zones. Automatic approvals are given by the government for setting up 100% Export Oriented Units. Incentives and facilities available under the EOU scheme include concessional rent for the lease of industrial plots, preferential power allocation and supply, exemption from import duty for capital goods and raw materials for power sector industries as well as for trading companies primarily engaged in export activity. Other incentives include:

- duty-free imports of raw materials and components;

- tax holidays for a period of five continuous years in the first eight years from the year of commencement of production;

- exemption from taxes on export earnings even after the period of tax holiday;

- exemption from central and state taxes on production and sale.

Further details on taxes and exemption are available online at www.incometaxindia.gov.in.

NETWORKING ORGANIZATIONS

The majority of businesses in India belong to a local or national Chamber of Commerce or other networking organization. These organizations are a good source of expert advice and information. They offer a forum for the generation of ideas, exchange of views and furthering business contacts in India. They regularly hold trade fairs and seminars.

Some of the major national organizations include:

1. The Associated Chambers of Commerce and Industry of India (ASSOCHAM)

Established in 1920, ASSOCHAM is one of India's premier chambers of commerce with a membership of 200,000 companies. As an industry body, ASSOCHAM represents the interests of industry and trade, works with government on policy issues and interacts with counterpart international organizations to promote bilateral economic issues. ASSOCHAM is represented on all national and local levels.
www.assocham.org

2. Federation of Indian Chambers of Commerce and Industry (FICCI)

FICCI campaigns for free enterprises in India. It has nationwide membership of over 1,500 companies and over 500 chambers of commerce and business associations. FICCI speaks directly and indirectly for over 250,000 businesses in India. ww.ficci.com

3. The American Chamber of Commerce in India (AMCHAM)

AMCHAM is an association of American business organizations in India. The organization is accredited by the Chamber of Commerce of USA, Washington DC, USA. It is also a member of the Asia Pacific Council of American Chambers (APCAC). AMCHAM promotes investment by US companies in India. www.amchamindia.com

4. Confederation of Indian Companies (CII)

Another powerful body in India, CII works and campaigns for the growth of industry in India. It has several regional chapters. www.ciionline.org

5. Federation of Indian Micro and Small and Medium Enterprises (FISME)

Another powerful advocate for small and medium enterprises in India. It has several local chapters and keeps its members informed about new development in the local marketplaces through circulars, e-mails and meetings. www.fisme.org.in

8
Money

BRINGING MONEY TO INDIA

It is probably best to bring at least £200 to £300 (bare minimum!) in cash and the rest in travellers' cheques from your home country that can be paid into the account of a (highly trusted) colleague, who will then give you the equivalent in rupees (less bank charges) to get yourself started until both your bank account is activated and your first pay packet comes through. Your company may be prepared to advance you several months' salary, but this is of no help if there are difficulties activating your bank account. While your ATM card from your home country **will** work in India, it is best to save it for emergencies. You will be charged for using it and also it can be blocked after just a couple of transactions, if your bank in the West is unaware that you are going to use it in India and they assume it has been stolen.

MONEY TRANSFER TO INDIA

Once you have opened your Indian bank account, you can transfer money using direct transfer (telegraphic or SWIFT) from your account in your home country. ICICI bank branches abroad offer free money transfer (over a certain limit) to Indian bank accounts. These may not be suitable for use in an emergency as it will take around three to four working days for money to reach your Indian account.

International Demand Drafts can also be purchased at banks abroad. However, they take a few days to clear in India, too.

Apart from banks and financial institutions, quick money transfer to India can also be made online or by telephone through money transfer companies. Some of them are:

- Western Union Money Transfer: www.westernunion.com;
- Money Gram International: www.moneygram.com;
- IKobo Money Transfer: www.ikobo.com;
- Cash2India: www.Cash2india.com;
- Remit2India: www.Remit2india.com;
- Samachar Money Transfer: www.moneytransfer.samachar.com;
- Times of Money: www.Timesofmoney.com;
- Wells Fargo International Money Transfer: www.wellsfargo.com;
- Travellers Express: www.travellersxpress.com.

Western Union and Money Gram transfer money immediately, but charge a hefty commission. Both have plenty of agents in India where cash can be collected.

BANKS IN INDIA

The banking system in India has a lot in common with that in Britain, so you will not find the adjustment too difficult. However, it is worth bearing a few points in mind and a little patience is required in the early stages.

State and private banks

In India there are nationalized banks (government owned), for example the Canara Bank and the State Bank of India and also independent private Indian banks such as ICICI, HDFC and UTI, as well as foreign banks such as HSBC, ABN-AMRO, etc. In common with other government employees, the staff of nationalized banks are sometimes accused (perhaps unfairly) of being less dedicated and hard-working than private sector employees whose jobs may depend on their performance (Indians refer to this as the 'hire and fire' system). In India, the banks can be separated into different groups. They each have their own dedicated target market. A few of them (usually nationalized) only work in rural sectors while others work both the rural as well as urban sectors. Some private banks only operate in cities.

However, after setting up bank accounts in both the government and the private sector, we have found them equally vexing! While it is probably fair to say that the privately-run banks have plusher interiors, smarter, younger employees, more ATMs and newer computers, the state banks are now rapidly modernising and have also started to improve their branches and install ATMs. Some private banks have introduced banking with a coffee. They have linked up with local cafés and remain open offering full banking facilities with a coffee till late in the evening. The majority of the banks are also open on Saturdays.

Private banks will also deliver/collect cash or other documents at your home. You'll never need to visit a branch after opening an account. They will send their messenger to fetch or bring your documents, or your personal manager will visit you. This of course will depend on how much you bank with them.

First steps to setting up an account

When you are ready to set up your first bank account, you will probably be assisted by your company who will put you in contact with a personal banker. This may seem to be a simple act of helpfulness on the part of your HR department, but actually there is an ulterior motive. Indian companies frequently only deal with one or two banks, with whom they have an agreement to give employees special privileges. This may mean that the company's employees have a certain free overdraft limit, privileges in obtaining a loan, or will not be charged for using another bank's ATMs to withdraw cash. This is quite different from the situation in the West, where you can freely set up an account with whichever bank you choose and your account will merely be credited with your wage.

You may be concerned that because of this state of affairs you cannot set up your account with an international bank that will let you transfer money to your home country free of charge (HSBC is currently one of the few international banks with a growing presence in India). However, the situation is really not that problematic, because major Indian high street banks (ICICI and HDFC for example) also have branches abroad. It is a good idea to confirm that the Indian bank you will set up your account with has branches in your home country, either through the bank's website or via your company's personal banker. The ICICI bank currently has five branches in Britain as well as a strong internet presence. HSBC also permits you to open an Indian bank account in your home country. The staff can assist you to set up an account via which you can transfer money to and from India free of charge.

Although HSBC (and to a lesser extent, Barclays) are doing business in India, there are so few branches per city in India that it is much better to save with India's high street banks which probably have branches within walking distance (or at most a short autorickshaw drive) from your apartment. Some private banks require you to keep 10.000 rupees in at all times whilst nationalized banks insist on being introduced by an existing account holder. As an expatriate, Indian banks will only open a Non Resident Other (NRO) bank account.

Use of ATMs

When setting up your bank accounts in India you may be surprised to find out that you are permitted to make six ATM withdrawals per month free of charge. Another slight difference is that some of the ATMs in India are not 24 hour, but only stay open until 11 pm under the supervision of an armed security guard who allows just two customers near an ATM at a time. The daily withdrawal limit from an ATM is currently 25,000 rupees, with a maximum individual withdrawal of 10,000 rupees, so if you wish to withdraw the maximum amount then you must withdraw 10,000 then 10,000 then 5,000.

You may also find the cash machine infinitely preferable to the queues and forms involved in over-the-counter transactions, especially considering the poor overlap between bank opening hours and Indian working/commuting hours. Some large international companies (such as Infosys, Wipro, General Electric) have ATM machines on-site at their Indian facilities, and this trend will probably continue.

Opening a bank account

When the personal banker meets you to set up your account, you have to fill in just one or two simple forms, provide supporting documents (see below) and then you will immediately be given a welcome pack with your cheque book, a debit card, PIN (for the debit card) and username and password for internet banking (you must re-assign these online to begin internet banking). But beware: your debit card may not work and your bank account may still not be active if your signature doesn't **exactly** match the one you have provided on a photocopy of your passport. You should keep checking via your personal banker or the bank's telephone helpline, or even in person at your bank. This difficulty may not come to light until your application form is processed at the bank's corporate head office a few days later: even though your personal banker has deemed your signature acceptable, it may still not get through the system. While you may feel like pulling out your hair and screaming, this is not the fault of your bank or your personal banker, but rather a consequence of the banking regulations in India. Not being able to reproduce your own signature can become embarrassing when you are trying to put down a deposit for a flat and don't want to keep borrowing from your colleagues, or else be charged excessively for transferring money from your home country. But don't despair! If you explain the situation to your head of human resources, a simple phone call to his/her contact at the bank is sometimes enough to clear the problem and get your account activated.

Another difficulty to arise from the issue of signature-matching is that even if your bank account has been activated, if you wish to cash a cheque to yourself at the bank it may not be accepted without being cleared by a higher-level contact at the bank.

Documents required for opening a bank account in India for non Indians
1. Proof of identity Photocopy of the main page or pages of the passport which contains your name, date of birth, date and place of issue, expiry date, photograph and signature. Photocopy of valid visa. If your visa has expired then the visa extension issued by the FRO/FRRO will be accepted as a valid document.
2. Proof of address Indian address on your passport (if any) Bank statements Rental agreements A letter from your existing banker who has held an account in that branch for more than three months. The letter should clearly state your residential address. Letter from employer confirming your name and address. Utility bills Residence permit issued by FRRO/FRO Driving licence Letter from government authorities

Other banking products

Remember that if your bank advises you about which investments to make in order to minimize your tax burden, double-check their advice online by e-mailing the (reputable) company or organization whose scheme they propose you invest with. Make it very clear that you are a foreigner, not an Indian national (whom the banks usually deal with) and tread carefully because only a few schemes are open to foreigners and an accountant specializing in these matters may be required.

Also be aware that under current regulations only Indian citizens are permitted to buy stock directly. The only option for you as an expatriate is to invest in a mutual fund. The problem with investing in a rupee denominated mutual fund in India is that you have to take into account the fluctuation of the rupee with respect to your base currency, if you decide to leave India.

INCOME TAX PERMANENT ACCOUNT NUMBER (PAN)

You do not need a PAN (see Chapter 6) to open a bank account in India. However, you'll need to have a PAN to make deposits or withdrawals over 50,000 rupees. By law banks will deduct tax at source (TDS) on the interest accrued.

CREDIT CARDS AND PERSONAL LOANS

Private banks and some foreign banks in India have started to offer credit cards and personal loans to expatriates. The facility may be restricted to the duration of your visa. You'll need to contact your personal banker for these products as the application forms are slightly different. Banks in India have not yet started offering mortgage facilities to expatriates in India.

Although a well-heeled foreigner working for a reputable company is perfectly safe, you might be interested to learn that even some of the top high street banks in India have employed rogue debt collectors (usually people with criminal records) to persuade debtors to cough up on outstanding loans. In fact, in 2007 one of the major private banks was caught up in such a scandal when a man who owed the bank money was beaten to death by a hired debt collector.

However, provided you keep records of all your financial transactions your banking experience in India should be a smooth one, and with the help of the internet (don't trust wireless connections) and the ATM you may actually enjoy it!

9
Housing

A great place to stay can substantially enrich your life in a foreign country. It can provide the environment to work, relax and bring up a family. When you first arrive in India, you are likely to be accommodated in a hotel or guest house provided by your company. Typically you may be given up to one month, possibly with the facility of a car and driver, in which to find your own apartment. This is a good time to investigate different locations by car and get advice from your workmates about which areas of your city are the best places to live in, yet are close enough for your daily commute.

FINDING A PLACE

For single men and women the majority of companies in India will provide accommodation in a serviced apartment. This is a modest three- to four-roomed flat and usually comes with a housekeeping service. Your company may even have housing facilities established for their expatriate personnel. If your company is unable to find you a house they will be able to advise on rental properties nearby. Your Indian colleagues may be moonlighting as property consultants in the city.

House hunting in India is similar to anywhere else in the world. You can look for housing through an accommodation (rental) agency, through newspapers or online. Increasing numbers of landlords, keen to let their properties to expatriates have started advertising online. Popular websites that carry accommodation listings include: www.suleka.com and www.indiaabroad.com.

Accommodation and marital status

You may be surprised to find that in India your marital status is a consideration when you are looking for an apartment. The difficulty comes if you are a bachelor, or a spinster in which case you may need someone to vouch for you. In India bachelors are seen as boozing, womanizing, partying, untidy and noisy trouble-makers who will carry out all sorts of unsavoury activities with their doors open in full view of respectable Indian families! For the same reason, you may find it hard to get a cleaning lady when it emerges that you are a bachelor, unless you can get someone to vouch for your good character. At this point it must be emphasized that in India female friends cannot visit your apartment, no matter how innocently, without arousing suspicion. The degree of this moral correctness may vary from one city to another, but one must always remember that in India a good reputation is of paramount importance.

Private house or apartment

Your choice of apartment or a house will depend on several factors, including proximity to the workplace, proximity to shops and/or the city centre, marital status and level of monthly rent. If you are earning a high enough salary, you may elect to employ a driver who will provide a taxi-style service to and from work. On your starting salary, you may prefer to either live close to work and then travel by auto (provided that autorickshaws travel that route – sometimes big companies are too far from the busy routes where autorickshaw drivers are guaranteed a return fare). Most employees choose the company buses which cover a wide variety of routes to work. The company bus will take a little longer for your daily commute than a car or auto, because it must pick up passengers over a circuitous route, but is cheap, reliable and relatively safe. However, you are inevitably limited to certain residential areas which are on the bus route and are not prohibitively far from the workplace. Many big companies in India are on the outskirts of towns and your commute may be from 40 to even 90 minutes each way.

Unfortunately, because so many workers are joining the commute to the edge-of-town companies, the popular residential areas can be over-crowded. You will have to find your own balance between a long commute to a peaceful area and a short commute to a polluted, noisy district where you can barely cross the road to the supermarket without being knocked down by traffic! If you are a really wily commuter, then with the help of your boss, head of HR or workmates you can sometimes find a nice place at a reasonable price close to work. A short commute makes a lot of sense, except you may also need to consider how close you are to shops and entertainment at the weekend. You are likely to go to your favourite bar or restaurant in the city centre or watch some Hindi or local-language movies with friends, but you may only be able to watch the latest Hollywood film in English. City centre accommodation is often costly, as well as a long commute, so you may choose to live somewhere equidistant between your workplace and the city centre.

If you search carefully you may be able to find a nice flat in a traditional Indian house, which is a flat-roofed two-storey building, often with the staircase on the outside. These buildings are cool and comfortable, and the modern ones are clean and pleasant to live in. Kitchens may be small but adequate and the traditional porcelain 'hole-in-the-ground' squatting toilets are increasingly being supplemented with, or even replaced by Western-style toilets. Most flats or apartments have a corner shop nearby which will have all the day-to-day staples such as onions, tomatoes, bottled water and soft drinks, milk and eggs, soap, shampoo and mosquito repellent.

Rent

Whether you live in a flat or a modern apartment block, you will usually find that your rent is made up of two components – the rent itself (currently in the region of 6,500 rupees per month for a reasonably-priced two-bedroomed flat) and a 'maintenance charge' of around 500 rupees per month which pays for the watchman. This rough figure of 7,000 rupees per month is currently valid for a reasonable apartment at an average commuting distance in a city like Hyderabad. The same price corresponds to a nice apartment in a cheaper area (but it may involve a longer commute) in an expensive city like Bangalore. However, there are no hard-and-fast rules and if your company happens to be one of those that isn't on the outskirts of town, or if you don't mind living away from the luxury areas or the city centre, you may find a bargain.

Look around for a few places with a range of rents. Do seek advice from your colleagues on the rents they pay and what rents you can expect. Keep on looking till you find the best one that suits you. There are always plenty of units available.

RENT AND DEPOSIT

The cost of rent is moderate by American or European standards. House rents for expatriates and their families vary considerably from one city to another. Rent is higher in Bombay and Delhi than in Calcutta, Madras and Bangalore. Rent is lower in other cities. Many of today's Indian professionals live in new apartment blocks with a car park beneath the building and a security guard, or at least a watchman at the gate to keep out unwanted salesmen.

It is common to have to pay a fee (perhaps in the region of 3,500 rupees or half a month's rent) for a housing broker (middleman) to negotiate/ find your accommodation. Ensure that you get a receipt for the housing broker's services, then you can reclaim the cost as part of your company's relocation package. Your landlord will also require you to put down a deposit. Remember the golden rule: in India **never** pay for anything without a receipt!

Houses in India are let to individuals on an 11-month basis (this avoids legal problems for the landlord) with a tenancy agreement. A rental deposit is common. The size of the deposit varies from one city to another and while you may only need to pay one or two months' rent in advance in Hyderabad, Bangalore is notorious for requiring up to ten months' rent in advance! This phenomenon is usually blamed not just on the recent housing boom, but also on the willingness of software engineers with more money than sense to pay outrageous prices. You may be asked (via a housing broker or helpful colleague) whether you require a contract from your landlord (who may not speak English). It is best to have a housing contract. In India housing contracts are on government 'stamp paper' and it will usually state mutually agreed terms and conditions of the rented property.

It is also advisable to have a housing contract in order to facilitate the legal requirement of getting a PAN card (see Chapter 6), which gives you a 'social security' number, although your company may provide an alternative proof of address. However, you may prefer not to have a housing contract if the deposit is small and you would like the freedom to leave suddenly if your accommodation or job is unsatisfactory. Furthermore, your landlord may not wish to provide a contract if he is dodging taxes himself!

ELECTRICITY AND WATER PROBLEMS

Electricity and water supply are unreliable and shortages are a common problem in India. Random blackouts are common during the peak summer months and you can expect daily unannounced power cuts (sometimes up to four hours a day) in many major cities.

It is best to buy an Uninterrupted Power Supply (UPS) – a crude form of back up supply to protect your equipment from power failure or buy petrol operated portable power generators. They are usually available for around 10,000 rupees. Transformers to convert foreign appliances to the Indian power cycle are available locally.

Indian cities have a restricted water supply, usually for two to four hours a day. The majority of houses have an underground tank to store tap water and an overhead tank to distribute water around the house. You can also buy water for household purposes from private water supply companies for about 400 rupees a tank.

However, it is best to make sure you have bottled drinking water or a big inverted water-container, with a tap in your kitchen. After you have paid an initial deposit, your local corner shop will refill the water-container for a small payment.

BRINGING YOUR HOUSEHOLD GOODS INTO INDIA

A lot of expatriates arrive in India with a large amount of household goods. We advise against this. The majority of Western electrical goods have compatibility problems in India and Indian conditions may not suit the product. Repairs may be difficult. You'll also incur shipping costs and the hassle of customs clearance.

Most electrical appliances are now produced in India, often with foreign collaboration. Besides, selling a local product will be a lot easier than foreign brands when you leave India. A list of products available in India is provided further on in this chapter.

FURNISHING THE HOUSE

In India apartments come 'unfurnished' and that means completely unfurnished! You will not find houses with wall-to-wall carpeting. You must buy everything from fans and fan-blades to the bed-frame, mattress, cooker, freezer, furniture and geyser to heat the water for your morning shower! In some cities, apartments do not even have sinks, and so you may try to negotiate with your landlord to fit sinks and perhaps a secure lock on your door before you move in.

Other things that you must buy before moving into your apartment are a bed (sometimes referred to as a 'cot') and mattress (sometimes referred to as a 'bed'). When you ask for a mattress, you may merely be offered a cheap cotton futon style mattress which will soon sag. If you pay more you can buy a good coir mattress or a sprung 'kurl-on' mattress. Even with the help of an Indian friend who can negotiate a lower price, you may be surprised to find that wooden bed frames do not come as cheaply in India as they do in the West! When you do find a carpenter's bed/furniture shop and the bed you have chosen is delivered (for a very small sum) you may find that it is poorly-crafted, with plenty of crevices for the cockroaches to hide in and you will never complain about IKEA again! Divans are widely available in India and are sometimes preferable to a conventional bed-frame, having no head-board for insects to hide in and with plenty of room for you to stretch your legs out. When you buy your bed, make sure that it is long enough and be adamant if the carpenter tries to persuade you that a bed of less than six feet in length is good enough!

You will also need a large bucket and jug (for washing), toilet paper (referred to as 'tissue roll') and liquid mosquito repellent, which comes with a plug-in vapourizer (popular brands are 'All-Out' and 'Good Knight') and last for 40 nights before you need to change the cartridge. Be aware that mosquito repellent has no effect on cockroaches and you should keep any food items sealed in plastic tubs or 'ziploc' plastic bags. Some people attempt to deter cockroaches by using a 'Lakshman Rekha', which is a piece of poison-impregnated chalk with which you draw a line on the floor that kills cockroaches on contact. However, it may be preferable not to use such strong poisons around the home, especially when lots of Indian cockroaches have the ability to fly if absolutely necessary. You may also be wise to wash cutlery and plates, rinsing with boiling water immediately before eating. Light-bulbs are available in both traditional and energy-saving forms, and fluorescent tube lights (which may not last very long!) are common, too.

Cooking

If you are planning on doing some cooking in your flat, you can either buy a gas stove with refillable cylinder, or a one- or two-ring electric stove. A popular cooking medium is gas, available in portable cylinders. Gas can be dangerous (see below), but if you prefer electric cooking the power ('current') may go off (especially at the weekend) when you are half way through boiling a pan of rice! For gas, you will need a 'connection' – where a dealer will supply you with the cylinders regularly. Government-owned oil and gas companies sell heavily subsidized gas, but have a year long waiting list for connection.

Private operators are now selling more expensive gas connections (usually at double the price of the nationalized operators). This involves a large deposit. It is advisable to get two cylinders at a time so that you have a backup when one cylinder runs out.

It is nice to get a fridge or fridge-freezer (again, these are more costly than in the West) if you want to have a supply of cold drinks during the heat of the summer, or to keep the remains of your cooking for reuse. The fridge in India also provides a place you can keep food items where the ants won't go.

A kettle is well worth buying along with a toaster, but these are also a little costlier than in the West. You can buy a geyser (electric water-heater) for your bathroom at a local electrical shop, along with your electric fans. Both will be fitted by the shop staff for a small charge, but don't be surprised if the geyser breaks down after a month or two. You may find the kettle useful as an emergency back up for hot water in the morning. Microwave ovens and televisions are costlier than in the West, but make you feel at home and you may be able to claim these items as part of your relocation expenses.

Warning!

There are a couple of potentially dangerous situations around the house you need to aware of; these involve gas and electricity.

Gas

You'll need to exercise a few precautions while dealing with gas cylinders. Do not ignore gas smells. Check the gas regulators and the rubber hose that connects stove and cylinder regularly. Change the rubber hose periodically and turn off the regulator when not in use.

Electricity

Do check the fuses and electrical wiring in the house before moving in. The majority of fuses in India have unsafe heavy conductor wires installed in them instead of proper fuse wire so that they never trip. Proper fuse wire will help protect your equipment when there is a power surge. Also be aware that some Indian houses have loose un-insulated electrical wiring that can be fatal when touched.

UTILITIES

Electricity

Electricity is provided by state run companies in India. You do not have to worry about an electricity connection. Your landlord should inform you about the meter reading before you move in. Your electricity bill will come once a month. It may be a good idea to check with the landlord, in advance, that all bills have been cleared before you move in. The electricity supply may be in the landlord's name and he may well come to collect the electricity money as well as the rent.

If you have made an agreement with the landlord to pay the bill, then you can pay the electricity bill directly at the state run electricity board collection centres or at a local post office 'e-SEVA' shop.

Water

Water facilities are provided by the local council and the tenant is responsible for the payment of bills. Your landlord should inform you about the meter reading before you move in. Your water bill will come once a month and can be paid at the local water board collection centres or at a local post office 'e-SEVA' shop.

Internet and cable

Getting an internet connection can usually be arranged, but if you deal with the national provider, BSNL, you may have to get an expensive landline connection. However, there are local companies that will fit a cable to provide the same service with a range of prices, depending on the speed of the connection and the quantity of data you may download in a month. To get a reasonable connection with unlimited downloads and 40 kbps (still not adequate for viewing clips on Youtube) you may have to pay around 600 to 800 rupees per month. Don't be surprised though if the boys from your internet company don't always come to collect your monthly payment and then cut you off, or if the connection goes off intermittently (this happens even with a BSNL connection). Small companies may of course go out of business at any time.

Telephones

Before you move into your apartment, check whether you can receive and make calls from mobile phones from inside your rooms. In some cases in parts of the block, especially amongst the lower floors, the signal strength may be very weak and you may only be able to make calls from out in the corridor. You can get a landline instead, but it is probably more troublesome than just finding another apartment or a different room in the same building where the signal is stronger. A standard landline is available immediately on demand from state run BSNL or private companies. You can also make international phone calls at a reasonable price (which may not be allowed in your usual phone contract) by visiting public telephone booths, located at almost every corner shop.

NEWSPAPERS

One of the easiest services to arrange is to have a newspaper delivered to your room every morning. This can be arranged at the corner shop for around 65 rupees per month. There are several English-language newspapers in most regions of India, with *The Times of India* (www.timesofindia.indiatimes.com) being the best-known. They provide an invaluable insight into not just the news but also the cultural perspectives and mindset of Indians, and come highly recommended.

DOMESTIC SERVICES

It is common in India for people to have domestic servants (remnants of the British Raj). Typical positions include cleaners, cooks, nannies, drivers, watchmen, gardeners and handyman. The majority of professional people have a cleaning lady (referred to as a 'servant-maid') or even a cook. Indian cleaning ladies will usually sweep up and clean your rooms and also wash your clothes (like *dhobis*, the outside washer-men who are likely to damage your clothes, so don't give anything precious to be washed). However, they often speak little English, will always try to negotiate a higher monthly salary with foreigners (1,000 to 1,500 rupees per month is typical, with a charge of six to eight rupees for each shirt or pair of trousers ironed). Check with your colleagues or neighbours before hiring anyone. It may be wise to keep the relationship on a business level and keep valuables securely stored.

Watchmen may be necessary where you live and they are often included with the house you rent.

It is common for domestic servants in India to expect an annual gift or a tip during the festive season. Indians are a very friendly people and if you show generosity from time to time, you will get friendly service and your cleaning lady or watchman will go the extra mile if you ever need a shirt ironing or other errands at the last minute.

Goods available in India

A wide range of household, electrical appliances and furniture are widely available in India. It is easy to have a piece of furniture custom made at a local carpenter store. Prices vary according to the wood you choose and the region you live in.

Furniture

Lounge set: 4,000–8,000 rupees for a three piece lounge set (three-seat couch, two side chairs and a table). More sophisticated upholstered furniture will be two or three times more expensive.

Beds: The majority of ready-made beds are short by Western standards. Custom-made queen-sized beds cost about 4,000–5,000 rupees.

Mattresses: Prices vary according to material. Single cotton futons (about five inches thick) are available for as low as 300 rupees, while single foam mattress can cost up to 3,000 rupees.

Dining table (with six chairs): They vary from 6,000–20,000 rupees depending on the size, quality and wood used.

Electrical appliances and household goods

Refrigerators: These are slightly more expensive than in the West. They come in various sizes. Small fridge-freezer combos with a capacity of 165 litres cost around 8,000 rupees. Medium-sized ones with 250 litres capacity cost around 15,000 rupees and larger multi door units cost over 23,000 rupees.

Gas stoves: Gas stoves are widely available. Ovens are not that popular because of the Indian style of cooking. Common two-burner table top gas stoves are available for 2,500 rupees. Gas stoves in India rarely come with pilot lights. You'll need to keep a lighter or a box of matches nearby.

Electric ovens: These are not that popular. They cost from 2,000 rupees.

Televisions and video players: These cost around 20,000 rupees for a standard 21 inch colour TV set. (Yes! Black and white TV sets are still sold in India!)
Video players cost about the same. DVD players are becoming popular.

Stereo: You can find a basic cassette/CD/tuner for about 5,000 rupees. Sets with additional features are expensive.

Washing machines: The most popular ones available are semi-automatic twin-tubs (one tub for washing and another for spin-drying). They start at 5,000 rupees and automatic ones start at 12,000 rupees. Dryers are not popular in India and the majority of people air-dry clothes outside.

Air conditioners: These are expensive. They cost about 18,000 rupees for window-type units. Split systems are expensive, too.

Air coolers: They blow humidified cool air into the room. They generally do not cool the room to the extent air conditioners can, but they will reduce the temperature in a room. Air coolers cost between 3,000–6,000 rupees, depending on size and cooling capacity.

Kitchen utensils: Lots of them are available at reasonable prices. The majority of them are sold by weight and the price varies according to the metal chosen. It is best to choose stainless steel utensils as they tend to last longer, do not get corroded and are hygienic. Utensils generally do not come with lids or handles. Lids are sold separately. Indian housewives use a claw style gripper to hold the hot utensils. These are also sold at utensil shops.

Household textiles: India has a variety of cotton textiles sold at reasonable prices. Bedspreads and cotton sheets come in a variety of designs and are often sold on the street. Prices range from 200 rupees for a single sheet to 400 rupees for double spreads. Fitted sheets are not popular. Curtains and drapes have to be made to order by a local tailor, but you have to supply the fabric. Hand woven carpets are popular.

BUYING PROPERTY IN INDIA

> **Note:** The Indian real estate market is still highly unregulated and disorganized. Much information supplied by brokers and estate agents should be seen simply as a tool to extract money from buyers. The regulations surrounding the purchase of property by foreign nationals is still a grey area and you are strongly advised to seek legal advice.

The Indian property market is booming along with its economy and you may wish to capitalize on this. The government of India has opened its economy cautiously. Foreign investment is being encouraged in areas where Indian nationals and the economy benefit.

Before you purchase any property, you need to be aware of foreign investment rules and policies including land ownership, property registration, repatriation of funds, legal and financial issues and more. Discuss these issues with a real estate solicitor before deciding to purchase.

Things to be aware of while dealing with property

- First get a good Indian lawyer experienced in property deals to represent you for a fee.

- Get the title, documents and possession certificates verified before signing anything or paying even a single rupee.

- **Do not agree to pay any portion of the sale price in cash.** Property deals in India usually employ tax-avoiding techniques referred to as white and black money. White money is paid by cheque and is taken as the sale price on record. Black money is paid in cash to lower tax, registration stamp duties or to lower capital gains liability for the seller.

It is advisable to ask your Indian bank to mediate the transaction. This is commonly known as 'Documentation Through Bank' (DTB) and anyone can utilize this service for a fee. The bank will hold your money safely until the sale is completed in all respects and until you are given possession of the property.

Property hotspots for expatriates

Coastal regions of Goa, Kerala and Karnataka are emerging as major property hotspots with an increase in the number of expatriates buying property. Seaside villas can be found for as low as 1,600,000 rupees (£20,000).

However, the prices of residential properties in major cities, particularly in some areas of Delhi, Mumbai and Bangalore have gone through the roof.

Mumbai, the commercial capital of India has always been the benchmark of the indicative real estate prices in India. Property prices in Mumbai are comparatively higher than in the rest of India. In the last few years, it has seen a record rise in property prices and can be compared with some of the highest real estate prices in the world.

In Bangalore, due to increasing investments by IT companies, there has been a growing demand for office space. This has consequently created an imbalance in supply and demand for residential properties. In recent times, property prices in Bangalore have been quite exorbitant.

Can foreign nationals buy property in India?

Indian regulations require a non-resident foreigner (visitor visa) to obtain prior permission from the Reserve Bank to purchase or lease any immovable property for a period exceeding five years. A foreign national who is 'a person resident in India' can purchase immovable property in India, but the person concerned would have to obtain the approvals and fulfil any requirements prescribed by other authorities, such as the state government concerned, etc.

Under the Indian government Foreign Exchange Management Act (FEMA) 'a person resident in India' is defined as a person residing in India for more than 182 days during the course of the preceding financial year and who has come to or stays in India either for taking up employment, carrying on a business or vocation in India or for any other purpose that would indicate his intention to stay in India for an uncertain period. The property purchased must be used for residential purposes only. Be aware that if you do earn rental income from property, the proceeds cannot be repatriated to your home country.

Further details on buying legalities of purchase of property by foreign nationals are available on www.rbi.org.in and www.femaonline.com.

10
Health

HEALTH CARE IN INDIA

One of the biggest concerns about your stay in India may be health. Many of you may worry what it would be like to stay in a country where you may have heard anecdotal evidence of well-publicized Indian health scares (e.g. 'Delhi belly') and fear that you could contract these too. The availability of proper health facilities, emergency care, medicines or difficult doctor-patient relationships may also be a source of worry.

The majority of suburbs, work places and tourist places you frequent as an expatriate are clean and hygienic. If you exercise basic precautions (as explained in an earlier chapter) then you can continue to lead a normal, healthy life. You are unlikely to get anything more than a stomach upset or flu. Do bear in mind that you will be living in a country with a different climate, eating a different diet, and a country where social customs are completely different from your own. Do take extra precautions during your first few weeks in the country. It is necessary for you to understand the health system in India to get the best possible medical care when you need it.

Medical facilities in India can vary from region to region. Some of the big cities have hospitals that are as good as the best anywhere, while rural and poorer areas have crowded, insanitary hospitals. The concept of health insurance is still relatively new in India and most people pay their medical expenses from their pockets. Some of the private health care facilities in Indian cities can be comparable with the best in the world.

The hospitals are hygienic and are equipped with state-of-the-art facilities backed up by highly-qualified staff who speak good English. Medical tourism (see below) might well be the next big success story out of India after software/outsourcing.

India has made mixed advances with public health. Life expectancy has improved from 36 years in 1951 to 65 in 2000, while infant mortality dropped from 146 per thousand births to 70 in the same period. These figures still rate poorly by Western standards. While diseases like smallpox, polio and leprosy have been eradicated, others like malaria and tuberculosis are not fully contained. India has four doctors for every 10,000 people, compared with 27 in the United States, according to the World Bank.

One of the great advantages of the Indian medical system is its informality and affordability: the pharmacist can prescribe a wide variety of generic medicines over the counter. Similar medicines elsewhere would be branded by big companies and available only with a doctor's prescription. Doctors' visits are relatively cheap as are hospitalisation costs, giving rise to the growth of medical tourism. A single tetanus shot costs 50 dollars in USA, but 15 cents in India, while heart surgery costs £15,000 in the UK but only £2,500 in India.

INDIAN HEALTH SYSTEM

India has both public and private health sectors. However, the quality of facilities and service in the public sector is poor and the majority of Indians do not use the 'free' government hospitals. As an expatriate working in India you'll probably be covered by your employer's group medical insurance. If your employer does not provide this then it is advisable to have private medical insurance, even though health care costs are reasonable in India compared with US, UK or Europe. If you do not have medical insurance from your home country, you can purchase it India from several insurance companies.

MEDICAL FACILITIES

Private medical clinics will probably be your first point of contact for minor medical treatments. Indian towns and cities have plenty of private medical clinics. It is a good idea to find a local doctor you like and trust as soon as possible after you arrive, before you have a need. It is advisable to get recommendations from your Indian friends and colleagues. Also, identify a good hospital for emergency treatment. Appendix 5 lists some of the hospitals that expatriates prefer in different cities in India. Please be aware that sometimes, the 'best hospital' in the city may be three hours away in an ambulance during the busy rush hour. Air ambulance services do not exist in Indian cities. A number of hospital chains have been set up recently, offering better quality care. If you do have to go to a hospital for a short stay or an operation, make sure you take someone with you as you may have to purchase supplies during your stay in the hospital.

COUNSELLING

Most large companies have an in house counsellor (usually somebody from HR department). Private counsellors and psychotherapists are rare in India but are listed in the Yellow Pages. Most hospitals have in-house or on-call psychiatrists who double-up as counsellors.

VACCINATIONS REQUIRED

The following vaccinations are advised for India: diphtheria, hepatitis A, hepatitis B, rabies, meningitis, polio, tetanus and typhoid. It is worth getting the vaccinations in your home country before you leave for India. It is also worth taking anti-malarial tablets. A full list of necessary/recommended vaccinations for India can be found at www.fco.gov.uk.

DENTISTS

Dental treatment in India is inexpensive compared with Western countries. Major towns and cities have plenty of well-equipped, private dental clinics run by well-experienced dentists (check Yellow Pages). There are also specialist dental hospitals in major cities and towns. The cost of dental treatment varies from around US$10 for a routine check up to around US$100 for root canal treatment. You may also be covered by your employer for dental treatment.

PHARMACIES

There is no shortage of them and you can find several pharmacies in almost every corner of the city. Pharmacy chains are beginning to appear all over India. The majority of them are open from 9 am until 10 pm. Major towns and cities have 24-hour pharmacies and they are listed in the Yellow Pages.

The cost of medication is very reasonable. In India many pharmacies are often run without the presence of a qualified pharmacist and often drugs (including valium, antibiotics and several other controlled medications) are dispensed without a prescription from a doctor.

OPTICIANS

Again, like pharmacists, there is no shortage of opticians and you can find several in almost every corner of the city. Most of them are listed in Yellow Pages. Opticians are open from 9 am till 9 pm.

Opticians charge a nominal fee for an eye test which is usually refunded if you buy glasses from them. Prices are very reasonable compared with Western countries. However, the cost of glasses and contact lenses varies from brand to brand and shop to shop with ones in inner cities and towns generally cheaper than those in more rural areas.

HEALTH INSURANCE

The concept is relatively new in India and the majority of Indians pay for their medical expenses from their pockets. Your health expenses may be covered by your company's group medical insurance. Do check with your employer first to ensure that you are fully covered for any unexpected medical treatments in India. Should you need private health insurance then there are a number of companies offering various policies. The number of companies offering health insurance has risen rapidly in recent years with the majority of them co-owned by Western insurance companies. Most health insurance packages cover the entire family whilst you are in India. Premiums usually start from 10,000 rupees a year and vary according to the level of cover chosen and number of adults included in the policy. Under Indian taxation law, premiums paid into health insurance can be claimed back from income tax.

As a private patient you can often choose when and where treatment will take place. The insurance companies have links with accredited hospitals where you can take advantage of 'cashless' medical treatment paid by the insurance company. However, should you wish to go to a hospital of your choice then you may have to pay first and get the monies reimbursed from the insurance companies. Certain illnesses (e.g. HIV, self injury, drug/alcohol induced, etc.) may not be covered by the private medical insurance policy and these will be explained in the policy documents.

The following companies offer insurance to expatriates residing in India:

- ICICI Lombard: www.icicilombard.com, tel: 1800 222 555;
- Bajaj Allianz: www.bajajallianz.com, tel: 1800 225 858;
- Royal Sundaram: www.royalsundaram.in, tel: 1800 345 8899.

HEALTH ISSUES IN INDIA

Although you are unlikely to catch anything more serious than flu or a stomach bug, the following are some of the health issues that you need to be aware of.

Malaria: There has been a resurgence of malaria in India in recent years. Malaria is caused by a parasite called plasmodium and is transmitted by mosquitoes. Symptoms of malaria include fever, headache and vomiting, and usually appear within two weeks after the mosquito bite. If not treated, malaria can quickly become fatal. Protection from mosquitoes and anti-malaria tablets are strongly recommended.

Chikungunya fever: There have been several reports of Chikungunya fever from various parts of India. It is a viral infection transmitted by mosquito bites. Symptoms include fever, joint pains, muscle aches, headache and a rash. The disease is not fatal, but causes a lot of physical inconvenience. Protection from mosquitoes is strongly recommended.

Typhoid: Regular outbreaks of typhoid are reported in India. It is mainly spread through contaminated food, drinks and water and is life threatening. Vaccinations are available for typhoid.

Rabies: This is another major health concern. It is estimated that one person dies from rabies every 30 seconds in India. Stray dogs are mainly responsible for the transmission of rabies to humans. Vaccination is strongly recommended.

Dengue: There have been reports of outbreaks of Dengue fever in Delhi and surrounding regions. Dengue is a mosquito-borne viral disease. It is transmitted by Aedes mosquitoes that bite primarily in the daytime and favour densely populated urban areas during the rainy season. At present, there are no vaccinations available for the Dengue fever. Protection from mosquitoes is strongly recommended.

Conjunctivitis: Conjuctivitis (Pink Eye) outbreaks are reported frequently around India. Most outbreaks of conjunctivitis are caused by enteroviruses or adenoviruses. In the majority of cases, the illness resolves uneventfully, but causes mild discomfort.

HIV (Human Immunodeficiency Virus): HIV infection is reported to be growing at an alarming rate in India, but expatriates are not at risk unless they have unprotected sexual contacts or receive injections or blood transfusions.

AYURVEDA

Another feature of India is the presence of many traditional medical systems that enjoy almost equal footing with Western medicine in the eyes of many Indians. The ancient Indian medical system of *Ayurveda* is the best known. It is still very popular and in daily use by millions of

Indians. The word *Ayurveda* means 'knowledge of life' in Sanskrit and comes from the word *ayus* meaning 'life' and *veda* meaning 'knowledge'. Hindus believe that *Ayurveda* is a divine revelation of the God Lord Brahma. The main beliefs of *Ayurveda* revolve around the theory that good health exists when there is a proper balance between three fundamental *doshas* (elements) called *Vata* (impulse), *Pitta* (heat or energy) and *Kapha* (fluids) and their disequilibrium causes ill health. The treatment to the ill health mainly comprises the use of powders, tablets and medicated oils prepared from natural herbs, plants and minerals. *Ayurvedic* doctors and medicines are regulated by the Indian government.

Ayurvedic centres in India

There are various centres/hospitals across the country, which provide *Ayurvedic* treatment. Kerala is the most famous destination for *Ayurvedic* treatment in India. There are several *Ayurvedic* clinics in almost every town and city. The centres are run by accredited *Ayurvedic* doctors who diagnose and dispense medicines. *Ayurvedic* medicines are expensive compared with Western medicines in India.

OTHER SYSTEMS OF MEDICINES

Other forms of traditional medicine include *Siddha* (the southern Indian equivalent of *Ayurveda*), *Unani* (Greek medicine popularized by the Muslim invaders), homeopathy and naturopathy. There are also plenty of quacks and snake-oil salesmen one should avoid.

MEDICAL TOURISM IN INDIA

This is another growing concept where people are visiting India for affordable medical treatment sometimes combining tourism. The most common treatments are heart surgery, eye care, knee transplant, spinal treatment, cosmetic surgery and dental care. The reasons behind the growth in medical tourism is quality private healthcare in India and low cost of treatment. Another factor contributing to 'medical tourism' is that in India you don't have to deal with a bloated medical bureaucracy that is a fact of life in Western countries. India has come a long way since the days when the rich travelled overseas for treatment. But sadly, there is a disturbing trend emerging where some of the poor Indians cannot afford proper medical treatment.

Since this is a new phenomenon, you need to be aware of certain aspects regarding insurance and legalities. Obviously, insurance companies in India will not provide cover for you unless you are a resident and working in India (see Chapter 4). As a medical tourist you'll need to check with your insurance provider whether treatment at a recognized hospital in India is covered by your policy. If not, then you will have to bear the expense of your treatment. However, the cost of treatment will be much less than the equivalent treatment in a hospital in the West.

The table below compares the cost of health treatments in India and the UK.

Treatment	UK (US$) approx.	India (US$) approx.
Open heart surgery	30,000	5,000
Complex spinal surgery with implants	13,000	4,600
Simple spinal surgery	6,500	2,300
Liver transplant	300,000	60,000
Cataract surgery	4,000	1,000
Root canal	4,000	100
Dental implants	2,000	400
Metal free bridge	5,000	500

11
Education

In the Indian subcontinent there is a long tradition of respect for a good education. Even in 700 BC, Taxila was established as a centre of learning and by AD 450, the University at Nalanda (in Bihar) attracted scholars from around the world. In today's India, education is becoming more important than ever. Because of the importance of a good education to give children a decent chance in life, schools, colleges and other educational institutions have become big business in India. The competition between schools is now so intense that large billboards around Indian cities proclaim that their school gives classes in karate, swimming and dancing as well as a good education, or display photos of their students who topped the year's state exams together with their subjects and grades. While Indian education can undoubtedly be very good, there are plenty of cases of people from a rural background (in a regional-language medium) who are educated to Masters level but speak English poorly (although quite understandably) and seem to have little idea of the world outside the Indian subcontinent.

A recent World Bank report states that in India there are more than 740,000 schools with around 3.6 million teachers. There are more than 175 universities offering undergraduate and postgraduate courses and about 6,000 colleges affiliated to these universities.

EDUCATION IN INDIA

The overall educational structure in India is referred to as the Ten + Two + Three (10 + 2 + 3) style. The first ten years provide general school education for all students. The '+2' is the senior, higher secondary or the pre-university stage which enables students to move into academic and vocational streams. The last stage involves graduate education, usually in a college, where the student goes for further studies in a chosen subject field.

Admission into India's education system is extremely complex, with reservation for castes, religions and various alternative scholarships. Entrance examinations, both at national and state level exist which can provide a route to a good university or institute. Education counselling agencies have sprung up to guide young students through the system, as have bureaus that promise places at top universities in Western countries (although these are usually very low-level academic institutes) to those who have not achieved a high enough grade for a merit placement in India. Qualifications abroad also have a high status, and in Europe the courses are often shorter than those in India. The recruitment bureaus charge commission on top of the fees Western universities charge to foreign students, in order to milk solicitous parents.

INDIA'S RESERVATION SYSTEM

Educational institutions in India are forced to comply with its Reservation System which was started during its independence, that gives preference for an increased number of places in colleges and universities and also in employment for the so-called 'backward castes'. The upshot of this system is that the exam scores required to gain entrance into further education are much lower for scheduled/backward castes and tribes than they are for higher castes such as Brahmins. Many students with very poor marks manage to get admissions into educational institutions, while students with extremely good marks are left out. This is the cause of a great deal of resentment because the initial campaigners for reservation had never intended the unrealistically high quotas set aside for the lower castes to continue for so long.

The politicians are afraid to redress the balance for fear of alienating the low-caste voters. As a result, the status quo will continue for the foreseeable future and Brahmin and other upper caste children often have to score over 90% to get into their academic institution of choice when for others a much lower mark is sufficient.

The intense competition for university and college places in India also means that tutoring and coaching are now services for which parents will pay excessive amounts, in the hope of helping secure their child's future. Sadly, the stresses of education (along with parental pressure to marry), have made the fear of disappointing exam results a leading cause of suicide amongst India's young people.

SCHOOLS

Free government schools are generally regarded as being so inferior that whenever possible, middle-class parents pay for their children's education. They often send their children to schools run by private or religious organizations – usually because of the quality of the school, rather than for any religious inclination. Sometimes these religious schools (whether Hindu, Muslim, Christian or another religion) provide places for children whose parents cannot afford a good education. In fact, for the very poor, the most important incentive to send their children to a religious school (for example, the ISKCON or Jesuit schools) is that a free lunch is provided for the children. However, in most cases a place at a religious school still costs money, and pupils may feel that they have to tolerate a degree of strict religious indoctrination. Nevertheless, the good exam grades and clear, crisp accent with which students learn to speak English at a good school ensure that demand for places remains strong.

Indian students take final school exams through various examination boards (similar to those in the UK). At pre-university college (which Indians enter a year earlier than in Britain) the system appears to resemble the American one, with each student knowing their 'GPA' or Grade Point Average. In common with the US, an Indian programme of further education often outlasts that in a British university by several years, making Indian MSc or PhD graduates considerably more mature than their British counterparts.

Probably the fairest assessment would be that the standard of education in India is highly variable, and so is the amount of money you must pay for it. There are all kinds of schools, including Christian (usually with names like St Xavier's, St John's or Christ College), Montessori (an education system pioneered by an Italian lady of the same name around 100 years ago) and the so-called 'International Schools' that may be attended by the children of foreigners working in India.

There are four stages of school education in India and they are primary, upper primary, secondary and higher secondary (or high school). Generally schooling lasts ten years. However, there are considerable differences between the various states and also nationally in terms of the structure during the first ten years of schooling.

The main types of schools boards in India are:

- the state government's Secondary Education Examination Board (SSLC). The majority of Indian schoolchildren are enrolled in this;
- the Central Board of Secondary Education (CBSE) board;
- the Council for the Indian School Certificate Examinations (ISCE) board;
- National Open School.

International Schools

There are also International Schools in India. They generally are well-funded, better-equipped and are culturally and ethnically diverse, but they are more expensive than regular schools. The exams conducted can have any of the syllabuses of the Indian Education Boards.

Admission procedures in schools

All schools (including International Schools) in India have their own admission procedures. Generally schools in India start admitting students from September to December for the next academic year. Usually, every school will make an announcement in the local newspapers with the dates they are open for admission. You'll then need to get the forms and prospectus from the institution, which may charge a fee. After submitting the form back to school (along with another set of fees) your child will have to undergo a written and oral entrance test as set by the school. The school will notify you of the result. If selected, then you'll need to confirm the admission, pay the fees and probably a contribution to a 'building fund' or a 'sports fund' (see below) after which your child will be admitted in the next academic year.

Building fund

In India a vast majority of schools and colleges demand donations and contribution to various funds from time to time. These are generally bribes hidden as parental contributions towards a fund, as accepting donations for admission is an offence under Indian Regulations. Many parents silently contribute to this in order to secure good education for their children.

PRE-UNIVERSITY COLLEGES

After secondary school, students move on to pre-university colleges in India. This enables students to move into academic and vocational streams where students choose science, commerce or arts subjects. Admission to pre-university colleges depends largely on the grade acquired in school. Most colleges also have an entrance test. Admission dates and details of entrance exams will be listed in the local newspapers after the announcement of the School Education Board results.

GRADUATE EDUCATION

At the graduate stage, the students go for further studies in their chosen field of subject. The most popular subjects are medicine and engineering (especially an eventual specialization in software engineering), which are regarded as a ticket to a comfortable and affluent life. Software engineers are seen as 'a good catch' to which parents will try to marry their daughters and have a good chance of getting a job abroad (with a salary that appears astronomical in India). This perception of the desirability of an education in medicine or engineering has meant that other technical subjects have been starved of the best quality students. Pure science professors (who have been used to exercising absolute power) are now having to work very hard to attract prospective students who can effectively pick and choose between institutions.

ADMISSIONS

To obtain a place in an engineering or medical college one has to go through a series of entrance tests at the state level. This is generally called the common entrance test and is conducted by the education authorities of the state.

Most of the colleges offer admission only to Indian students on the basis of their performance in a competitive entrance test, but all of them allow foreign students to join directly at a higher fee structure. The admission again will depend on your contribution to the 'building fund'.

CENTRES OF EXCELLENCE

If one intends to pursue research in science, technology or management, then India's national institutes are better equipped and funded than state-funded universities. Science and technology subjects are best tackled at institutes such as:

- IISc (Indian Institute of Science), Bangalore (and recently, Pune);

- IICT (Indian Institute of Chemical Technology), Hyderabad;

- NCBS (National Centre for Biological Sciences), Bangalore;

- BITS (Birla Institute of Technology and Science) at Pilani in Rajasthan (also with branches at Goa, Bangalore and soon Hyderabad);

- CCMB (Centre for Cellular and Molecular Biology) in Hyderabad; and NCL (National Chemical Laboratories), Pune.

For business, the six centres of excellence are: the 'IIMs': IIMA/B/C/L/I/K (Indian Institute of Management, Ahmedabad, Bangalore, Calcutta,

Lucknow, Indore and Kozhikode, and in the near future, Shillong [IIMS], respectively). The gold standard in India, at least in terms of status are the 'IITs', or Indian Institutes of Technology which can be attended (if your grades are outstanding) at centres such as Bombay (Mumbai), Kanpur, Madras (Chennai) and Kharagpur, Delhi, Guwahati and Roorkee. An IIT Master's degree is respected at least as much as an Oxford or Cambridge degree was in 1920s UK.

Further details about Indian education can be found at www.education.nic.in.

12
Leaving India

Leaving any country where you have lived for a long time can be a painful experience, but leaving a country that offers a distinctive experience like India can be especially difficult. Increased globalization means you may not miss India away from India. India was still an unknown entity a decade or so back, but not so any more.

You can see many *saree*-clad women in the malls and shopping centres anywhere in the world. Indian movies are screened in many cinemas globally and available as DVD rental almost everywhere. If you took a liking to Indian food, all the big cities around the world have many Indian restaurants, though the offering is mostly standard fare. If you took a liking to Indian cooking, just look at your local Yellow Pages or telephone directory for the location of Indian groceries. If Indian religion impressed you, you will find Hindu temples and cultural centres in many parts of the world. If you took a liking to the game of cricket that is so ubiquitous in India, you will find cricket leagues even in countries where cricket is unheard of. If you made close friends in India, you can stay in touch with them with all of the tools of modern telecommunications.

Bringing over the friends you made in India may be more difficult because visas are not so readily granted to Indians. Working in other countries, having worked for a considerable time in India may also prove challenging. If you have liked the informal atmosphere of India, you may find the work environment back home difficult. But if you hated the fact that people barge into your cubicle unannounced, you may be only too glad to be back home.

BEFORE YOU LEAVE

There will be a range of matters that you need to attend to before you leave India: some of these could be financial, like having to pay your bills and other dues, closing your bank accounts or terminating your lease. Some of these could be logistical like sending your belongings back home. Some of these could be emotional matters like having to say goodbye to your colleagues and go back to your country: a sorrowful task for many. Some students might not want to leave their colleges behind, deciding instead to stay for a second course and may wonder how to do that.

EXIT PERMITS

Before you leave India you may hear mixed messages about whether you need a document that is variously referred to as a 'no objection certificate', an 'exit permit', or less correctly an 'exit visa' in order to leave the country.

If you are leaving India on a date lying within the legal period of your visa (for example, a one year grant for an employment visa), then you do not have to worry about this and can leave, simply by turning up at the airport and catching your flight.

However, you **do** need an exit permit if you have outstayed/extended the period of your initial visa in India. Remember that you may be considered to have outstayed your visa, even if you have had a visa extension of six months from your city's main police station. Even if you have paid for your visa extension, filled in the necessary forms, supplied the necessary photos and a letter from your small local police station attesting that you have not committed any offence while in India, you are still not technically permitted to remain in India. The reason for this is that your extension permit duly signed and endorsed by your city's superintendent of police, is incomplete until permission to extend the visa is granted by the Indian government in Delhi.

We have often wondered whether one's application for an extension of visa ever reaches Delhi, but we have heard anecdotally that the sought-after confirmation of visa extension may be forthcoming after a year or perhaps 18 months! On the occasions when we have applied for such an extension and worried that in the remaining six months (the maximum extension of visa granted) no official confirmation from the central government arrived, the authorities have told us not to worry about such things.

Getting an exit permit

In fact, they were right and it does not turn out to be a problem, provided that you pay a courtesy call to your city's police station or visa office just a few days before leaving India. All you have to do is produce the stamped visa extension documents that the police gave you when they granted your extension (on a local government level) and ask for an exit permit. They will sign a note giving you permission to leave the country, with the ever-essential rubber stamp, and within a few minutes the job should be over.

Sometimes, in an emergency, an exit permit can be given at the airport just before you catch your flight if you have all the necessary visa extension forms from the police. This method is not recommended and although the airport police will probably grant your exit permit, it will be accompanied by a reprimand that in future you should do this at the city police station, not the airport!

TAX CLEARANCE CERTIFICATE

If you are leaving India permanently then a tax clearance certificate (No Objection Certificate) from the income tax department is also required to be given to the Indian immigration authorities at the port of exit. The certificate states that you have settled your tax liabilities at the time of departure and the income tax department has no objections to you leaving the country. Although rarely asked for, it is essential to have one.

To obtain this tax clearance certificate, you will have to apply for it on Form 30A at your local tax office (check Yellow Pages). This form requires the employer (through whom the non-resident/foreigner has earned income in India) to provide a guarantee to pay any taxes payable by the person leaving India, under the Indian Income Tax and Wealth Tax Act. The tax clearance certificate in Form 30B is issued almost immediately on receipt of Form 30A and has a specific period of validity.

CHANGING YOUR MONEY

If you have large sums of money in Indian rupees held in an Indian bank account, then it is advisable to transfer the money to your bank account in your home country electronically. Most banks transfer the money electronically in a couple of days. You'll need to walk into the branch and fill in a transfer remittance form. You'll also need to provide photocopies of your passport and Indian visa.

You can also change money into travellers' cheques or required currency at any foreign exchange (forex) bureau. You'll need to show your passport and Indian visa.

If you have a 'worldwide' ATM card issued by your bank in India, you may find it convenient to withdraw money in your home country. ATM cards usually have a daily withdrawal limit and often have withdrawal charges.

SENDING GOODS BACK HOME

While staying in India it is hard not to accumulate quite a collection of mementoes. Because of this occupational hazard, you may find that by the time you leave India the weight of your suitcases surpasses both your luggage allowance and the Olympic record for weightlifting! Do not worry, a relatively economical solution is provided by your city's main post office. The Indian post office, for a very reasonable charge (by Western standards) allows you to pack a sizable chest with your valuables for shipping to your home address in the West. Your possessions are expected to arrive home within a month, but do pack carefully because these chests will **not** be handled with care! Books may arrive bent and fragile items may be broken, so it is best to fill the chest mainly with clothes and non-breakable items.

Sending goods back home by airfreight is a lot quicker, but it is expensive as the airfreight companies charge you according to the weight. On the other hand, shipping companies charge according to size and this can work out a lot cheaper. However, they are slow. Expect it to take around three to four weeks or longer to send goods back to Europe by ship.

Check customs regulations in India and in your home country

Before buying goods to take back home check the customs regulations in India and your country as some items may be prohibited for export or may incur a customs duty in your home country.

Checklists before you go home
Income Tax Clearance Certificate (No Objection Certificate) See above.
Exit Permit (if required) See above.
1   Close bank accounts If you are leaving India permanently then notify the bank, withdraw your cash and transfer it back home. If you are planning to come back to India after some time then it may be worthwhile keeping the account open with a minimal deposit in it.
2   Close other accounts (mobile, telephone, gas, electricity, etc.) Do not forget to inform any other companies that you have a contract with and close your accounts with them. Also check whether you owe them money or are owed money by them.
3   Send money back home Do not take large sums of money back home as it is not safe and might violate customs regulations in your country. Try taking it back/sending it using the methods listed above.
4   Leave forwarding addresses Do not forget to leave a forwarding address with your company, landlord and any other parties concerned. This will also help get your mail redirected.

If you bear these points in mind then you can look forward to a peaceful trip home.

As they say in India, 'Happy Journey!'

Appendices

APPENDIX 1: DIALLING CODES

National dialling codes

Agra: 0562

Ahmedabad: 079

Amritsar: 0183

Bangalore: 080

Baroda: 0265

Bhopal: 0755

Bikaner: 0151

Chandigarh: 0172

Chennai: 044

Chandigarh: 0172

Coimbatore: 0422

Delhi (Region): 011

Dehradun: 135

Fathepur Sikri: 05619

Hyderabad: 040

Jaipur: 0141

Jullandar: 0181

Kanpur: 0512

Kolkata: 033

Lucknow: 0522

Mumbai: 022

Mysore: 0821

Mangalore: 0824

New Delhi: 011

Patna: 0612

Pune: 020

Pushkar: 0145

Rajkot: 0281

Simla: 0177

Srinagar: 0194

Surat: 0261

Udaipur: 0294

Vadodara: 0265

International dialling codes

Europe

Austria: 00 43

Belgium: 00 32

Cyprus: 00 357

Denmark: 00 45

Finland: 00 358

France: 00 33

Germany: 00 49

Greece: 00 30

Ireland: 00 353

Italy: 00 39

Netherlands: 00 31

Norway: 00 47

Poland: 00 48

Russian Federation: 00 7

Spain: 00 34

Sweden: 00 46

United Kingdom: 00 44

Other countries

Argentina: 00 54

Brazil: 00 55

Canada: 00 1

China: 00 86

Ghana: 00 233

Hong Kong: 00 852

India: 00 91

Israel: 00 972

Japan: 00 81

Kenya: 00 254

Korea (South): 00 82

Malaysia: 00 60

Mexico: 00 52

Nigeria: 00 234

Saudi Arabia: 00 966

Singapore: 00 65

South Africa: 00 27

UAE: 00 971

United States: 00 1

APPENDIX 2: DIPLOMATIC REPRESENTATION IN INDIA

Embassy of Argentina
B-8/9 Vasant Vihar
Paschimi Marg
New Delhi 110 057
Tel: +91-11-671345 or 671348 or 6882029; Fax: +91-11-3172373

Australian High Commission
No. 1/50 G Shantipath
Chanakyapuri
New Delhi 110 021
Tel: +91-11-41399900; Fax: +91-11-41494490
austhighcom.newdelhi@dfat.gov.au; www.india.embassy.gov.au

Australian Consulate in Mumbai
36 Maker Chambers VI
220 Nariman Point
Mumbai 400 021
Tel: +91-22-56692000; Fax: +91-22-56692005
dima.india@dfat.gov.au

Belgian Embassy
50-N Shantipath
Chanakyapuri PB 3
New Delhi 110021
Tel: +91-11-4108295, 6875728, 6889204, 6889851;
Fax: +91-11-6885821
NewDelhi@diplobel.org

Belgian Consulate in Mumbai

Morena 11
ML Dahanukar Marg
(Carmichael Road)
Mumbai 400026
Tel: +91-22-4958115, 4974302; Fax: +91-22-4950420
Bombay@diplobel.org

Embassy of Brazil

8 Aurangzeb Road
New Delhi 110011
Tel: +91-11-3017301; Fax: +91-11-3793684

Czech Embassy

50-M Niti Marg
Chanakyapuri
New Delhi 110021
Tel: +91-11-26110205 or 26110318; Fax: +91-11-26886221
newdelhi@embassy.mzv.cz; www.mfa.cz/newdelhi

Czech Consulate in Mumbai

5 G Deshmukh Marg
Mumbai 400 026
Tel: +91-22-24909456 or 24924484; Fax: +91-22-24950042
gkbombay@bom3.vsnl.net.in or bombay@embassy.mzv.cz;
www.mfa.cz/bombay

Royal Danish Embassy

11 Aurangzeb Road
New Delhi 110021
Tel: +91-11-3010900; Fax: +91-11-3792019
denmark@vsnl.com; www.denmarkindia.com

Royal Danish Consulate General in Mumbai
L & T House
Ballard Estate
NM Marg
Mumbai 400 001
Tel: +91-22-22614462; Fax: +91-22-22703749
danishconsulate@lth.ltindia.com

French Embassy
2/50E Shantipath
Chanakayapuri
New Delhi 110 011
Tel: +91-11-6118790 to 93; Fax: +91-11-6872305

German Embassy
No. 6 Block 50-G Shantipath
Chanakyapuri
New Delhi 110 021
Tel: +91-11-6871831; Fax: +91-11-6873117
www.germanembassy-india.org/

Italian Embassy
50-E Chandragupta Marg
Chanakyapuri
New Delhi 110 021
Tel: +91-11-26114355; Fax: +91-11-26873889
italemb@del3.vsnl.net.in; www.italembdelhi.com

Japanese Embassy
Plot No. 4 & 5 50-G Shantipath
Chanakyapuri
New Delhi 110021
Tel: +91-11-26876564, 26876581; Fax: +91-11-26885587
www.in.emb-japan.go.jp

Japanese Consulate in Kolkata (Calcutta)

55 MN Sen Lane
Tollygunge
Kolkata 700 040
Tel: +91-33-24211970; Fax: +91-33-24211971

Japanese Consulate in Chennai

No. 12/1 Cenetoph Road
1st Street Teynampet
Chennai 600 018
Tel: +91-44-24323860; Fax: +91-44-24323859

Japanese Consulate in Mumbai

No. 1 ML Dahanukar Marg
Cumballa Hill
Mumbai 400 026
Tel: +91-22-23517101; Fax: +91-22-23517120

High Commission of Malaysia, New Delhi

50-M Satya Marg
Chanakyapuri
New Delhi 110 021
Tel: +91-11-26111291; Fax: +91-11-26881538
maldelhi@kln.gov.my

Malaysian Consulate in Chennai

44 Tank Bund Road
Nungambakkam
Chennai 600 034
Tel: +091-44-28226888; Fax: +091-44-28226891
mwmadras@dataone.in

Royal Netherlands Embassy

6/50 F Shanti Path
Chanakyapuri
New Delhi 110 021
Tel: +91-11-24197600; Fax: +91-11-24197710
nde@minbuza.nl; www.mfa.nl/nde-en

Consulate-General of Netherlands in Mumbai

Forbes Building
Charanjit Rai Marg
Mumbai 400 001
Tel: +91-22-22194200; Fax: +91-22-22194230
bom@minbuza.nl

Consulate of Netherlands in Chennai

76 Venkata Krishan Road
Mandaveli
Chennai 600 028
Tel: +91-44-43535381; Fax: +91-44-24993272
honconsul.netherlands@gmail.com

Consulate of Netherlands in Kolkata

502 Mangalam-'A'
24 Hermanta Basu Sarani
Kolkata 700 001
Tel: +91-33-22204273; Fax: +91-33-22430165
nedconsl@cal2.vsnl.net.in

Royal Norwegian Embassy

50-C Shantipath
Chanakyapuri
New Delhi 110 021
Tel: 91-11-41779200; Fax: 91-11-41680145
emb.newdelhi@mfa.no; www.norwayemb.org.in

Embassy of the Sultanate of Oman

EP 10 & 11 Chandragupta Marg
Chanakyapuri
New Delhi 110 021
Tel: +91-11-26885622; Fax: +91-11-26885621
omandelhi@vsnl.com

High Commission of Singapore

N-88 Panchsheel Park
New Delhi 110 017
Tel: +91-11-51019801; Fax: +91-11-51019805
singhc_del@sgmfa.gov.sg; www.mfa.gov.sg/newdelhi

Consulate General of Singapore in Mumbai

101 10th floor Maker Chambers IV 222
Jamnalal Bajaj Road
Nariman Point
Mumbai 400 021
Tel: +91-22-22043205; Fax: +91-22-22855812
singcon_bom@sgmfa.gov.sg; www.mfa.gov.sg/mumbai

Consulate General of Singapore in Chennai

17-A North Boag Road
T Nagar
Chennai 600 017
Tel: +91-44-28158207–8; Fax: +91-44-28158209
singcon_maa@sgmfa.gov.sg; www.mfa.gov.sg/chennai

Embassy of the Slovak Republic

50M Niti Marg
Chanakyapuri
New Delhi 110021
Tel: +91-11-26889071; Fax: +91-11-26877941
skdelhi@giasdl01.vsnl.net.in

High Commission of South Africa
B-18 Vasant Marg
Vasant Vihar
New Delhi 110 057
Tel: +91-11-26149411; Fax: +91-11-26143605
highcommissioner@sahc-india.com; www.sahc-india.com/g_maite.html

Spanish Embassy in India
12 Prithviraj Road
New Delhi 110 011
Tel: +91-11-41293000; Fax: +91-11-41293020
embspain@vsnl.com

Embassy of Sweden
Nyaya Marg, Chanakyapuri
New Delhi 110 021
Tel: +91-11-24197100; Fax: +91-11-26885401
ambassaden.new-delhi@foreign.ministry.se;
www.swedenabroad.com/newdelhi

Swiss Embassy
PO Box 392
Nyaya Marg, Chanakyapuri
New Delhi 110 021
Tel: +91-11-26878372; Fax: +91-11-26873093
ndh.vertretung@eda.admin.ch; www.eda.admin.ch/newdelhi

Taiwanese Embassy
Taipei Economic and Cultural Center
12 Paschimi Marg, Vasant Vihar
New Delhi 110 057
Tel: +91-11-41662700; Fax: +91-11-6148480
ind@mofa.gov.tw

Embassy of the United Arab Emirates

EP-12 Chander Gupta Marg, Chanakyapuri
New Delhi 110 021
Tel: +91-11-26872937; Fax: +91-11-26877648
embassymirates@bol.net.in

Consulate General of the United Arab Emirates in Mumbai

No.7 Jolly Maker, Apartment No. 1
Cuffe Parade, Colaba
Mumbai 400 005
Tel: +91-22-22183021; Fax: +91-22-22180986
emarat@bom.vsnl.net.in

Embassy of the United States

Shantipath
Chanakyapuri
New Delhi 110021
Tel: +91-11-24198000; Fax: +91-11-24190017
ndcentral@state.gov; www.newdelhi.usembassy.gov

Consulate General of the United States in Chennai

220 Anna Salai Road
Chennai 600 006
Tel: +91-44-28574242; Fax: +91-44-28112020
chennaiNIV@state.gov,chennaiIV@state.gov;
www.chennai.usconsulate.gov

Consulate General of the United States in Kolkata

5/1 Ho Chi Minh Sarani
Kolkata 700 071
Tel: +91-33-39842400; Fax: +91-33-22822335
consularkolkata@state.gov; www.calcutta.usconsulate.gov

Consulate General of the United States in Mumbai
78 Bhulabhai Desai Road
Mumbai 400 026
Tel: +91-22-23633611; Fax: +91-22-23630350
MumbaiNIV@state.gov; www.mumbai.usconsulate.gov

APPENDIX 3: INDIAN EMBASSIES AND HIGH COMMISSIONS ABROAD

Argentina
Embassy of India
Avenida. Cordoba 950, 4th Floor
1054 Buenos Aires
Tel: +54-11-43934001, 43934156; Fax: +54-11-43934063
indemb@indembarg.org.ar; www.indembarg.org.ar

Australia
High Commission of India
3-5 Moonah Place
Yarralumla
Canberra ACT 2600
Australia
Tel: +61-2-62733999, 62733774; Fax: +61-2-62731308
hcicouns@bigpond.com; www.hcindia-au.org

Sydney
Consulate General of India
25 Bligh Street, Level 27
Sydney
New South Wales 2000
Australia
Tel: +61-2-92239500; Fax: +61-2-92239246
indianc@bigpond.com; www.indianconsulatesydney.org

Austria
Embassy of India
Kaerntnerring 2
A-1015
Tel: +43-1-5058666–9; Fax: +43-1-5059219
indemb@eoivien.vienna.at; www.indianembassy.at

Bahrain
Embassy of India
Building 182, Road 2608
Area 326, Ghudaibiya
PO Box No. 26106
Adliya – 326
Tel: +973-712683, 712785, 713832; Fax: +973-715527
hoc@indianembassy-bah-com; www.indianembassy-bah.com

Belgium
Embassy of India
217 Chaussee de Vleurgat
1050 Brussels
Tel: +32-2-6409140; Fax: +32-2-6489638
hoc@indembassy.be; www.indembassy.be

Brazil
Embassy of India
SHIS QL 08, Coj 08
Casa 01, Lago Sul, CEP 71.620/285
Brasilia, DF
Tel: +55-61-2484006 [4 lines]; Fax: +55-61-2485486
hoc@indianembassy.org.br; www.indianembassy.org.br

Canada
High Commission of India
10 Springfield Road
Ottawa
Canada
Tel: +1-613-7443751–3; Fax: +1-613-7440913
hicomind@hciottawa.ca; www.hciottawa.ca

Consulate General of India
Suite # 700, 365 Bloor Street East
Toronto
Ontario M4W 3 L4
Canada
Tel: +1-416-9600751–2; Fax: +1-416-9609812
cgindia@cgitoronto.ca; www.cgitoronto.ca

China
Embassy of India
1 Ritan Dong Lu
Beijing 100600
China
Tel: +86-10-65321908, 65631858; Fax: +86-10-65324684
webmaster@indianembassy.org.cn; www.indianembassy.org.cn

Czech Republic
Embassy of India
Valdstejnska 6
11800 Prague 1
Czech Republic
Tel: +420-257533490–3; Fax: +420-257533378
indembprague@bohem-net.cz; www.india.cz

Denmark
Embassy of India
Vangehusvej 15
2100 Copenhagen
Denmark
Tel: +45-39182888, 39299201; Fax: +45-39270218
indemb@email.dk; www.indian-embassy.dk

Finland

Embassy of India
2 A 8 Satamakatu
00160 Helsinki
Finland
Tel: +358-9-2289910; Fax: +358-9-6221208
eoihelsinki@indianembassy.fi; www.indianembassy.fi

France

Embassy of India
15 Rue Alfred Dehodencq
75016 Paris
France
Tel: +33-1-40507070; Fax: +33-1-40500996
eiparis.admin@wanadoo.fr; www.amb-inde.fr

Germany

Embassy of India
Tiergartenstrasse 17
10785 Berlin
Germany
Tel: +49-30-257950; Fax: +49-30-25795102
chancery@indianembassy; www.indianembassy.de

Ireland

Embassy of India
6 Leeson Park
Dublin -6
Ireland
Tel: +353-1-4970843; Fax: +353-1-4978074
indembassy@eircom.net; www.indianembassy.ie

Israel
Embassy of India
140 Hayarkon Street
PO Box 3368
Tel Aviv-61033
Tel: +972-3-5291999; Fax: +972-3-5291953
indemtel@indembassy.co.il

Italy
Embassy of India
Via XX Settembre 5
00187 Rome
Tel: +39-06-4884642–5; Fax: +39-06-4819539
admin.wing@indianembassy.it; www.indianembassy.it

Japan
Embassy of India
2-2-11 Kudan Minami
Chiyoda-ku
Tokyo – 102-0074
Japan
Tel: +81-3-32622391–7; Fax: +81-3-32344866
indembjp@gol.com

Korea (Republic of)
Embassy of India
37-3 Hannam-dong
Yongsan-ku
Seoul 140210
Republic of Korea
Tel: +82-2-7984257, 7984268; Fax: +82-2-7969534
eoiseoul@shinbiro.com; www.indembassy.or.kr

Kuwait

Embassy of India
Diplomatic Enclave
Arabian Gulf Street
PO Box No. 1450 – Safat
13015-Safat
Kuwait
Tel: +965-2530600, 2540612; Fax: +965-2525811
indem@qualitynet.net

Netherlands

Embassy of India
Buitenrustweg-2, 2517 KD
The Hague
Netherlands
Tel: +31-70-3469771; Fax: +31-70-3617072
fscultur@bart.nl; www.indianembassy.nl

New Zealand

180 Molesworth Street
PO Box 4045
Wellington
New Zealand
Tel: +64-4-4736390-91; Fax: +64-4-4990665
hicomind@xtra.co.nz; www.hicomind.org.nz

Norway

Embassy of India
Niels Juels Gate 30
0244 Oslo
Norway
Tel: +47-22552229, 22443194; Fax: +47-22440720
fscultur@bart.nl; www.indianembassy.nl

Oman

Embassy of India
PO Box 1727
Ruwi, Postal Code 112
Oman
Tel: +968-7714120; Fax: +968-7717503
indiamct@omantel.net.om; www.indemb-oman.org

Poland

Embassy of India
Ul. Rejtana 15, Flats 2-7
02-516 Warsaw
Poland
Tel: +48-22-8495800, 8496257; Fax: +48-22-8496705
goi@indem.it.pl

Portugal

Embassy of India
Rua Pero da Covilha 16
Restelo
1400 Lisbon
Portugal
Tel: +351-213041090; Fax: +351-213016576
hoc@indembassy-lisbon.org; www.indembassy-lisbon-org

Qatar

Embassy of India
No. 6 Al Jaleel Street
Al Hilal Area, PO Box 2788
Doha
Qatar
Tel: +974-4672021, 4674660; Fax: +974-4670448
indembdh@qatar.net.qa; www.indianembassy.gov.qa

Russian Federation
Embassy of India
6-8 Vorontsovo Polye
(Ulitsa Obukha)
Moscow
Russian Federation
Tel: +7-095-9170820, 7837535; Fax: +7-095-9752337
chocmos@com2com.ru; www.indianembassy.ru

Saudi Arabia
Embassy of India
PB No. 94387
Riyadh-11693
Saudi Arabia
Tel: +966-1-4884144, 4884691; Fax: +966-1-4884750
com@indianembassy.org.sa; www.indianembassy.org.sa

Slovak Republic
Embassy of India
Radlinskeho 2
811 02 Bratislava
Slovak Republic
Tel: +421-2-52931700; Fax: +421-2-52931690
eindia@slovanet.sk

Singapore
India House
31 Grange Road
Singapore – 239702
Tel: +65-67376777, 62382537; Fax: +65-67326909
indiahc@pacific.net.sg; www.embassyofindia.com

Spain

Calle Sanjose No. 23, 2nd Floor
PO Box No. 336
38002 Santa Cruz de Tenerife
Canary Islands
Spain
Tel: +34-22-341416, 243503; Fax: +34-22-289755

Sweden

Embassy of India
Adolf Fredriks Kyrkogata 12
Box 1340
111 83 Stockholm
Sweden
Tel: +46-8-107008, 4113212; Fax: +46-8-248505
information@indianembassy.se; www.indianembassy.se

Switzerland

Embassy of India
Kirchenfeldstrasse 28
3000 Berne 6
Switzerland
Tel: +41-31-3511110, 3511046; Fax: +41-31-3511557
India@spectraweb.ch

Thailand

Embassy of India
46 Soi Prasarnmitr
Soi 23
Sukhumvit Road
Bangkok 10110
Tel: +66-2-2580300-05; Fax: +66-2-2584627
indiaemb@mozart.inet.co.th; www.indiaemb.or.th

United Arab Emirates
Embassy of India
Plot No. 10, Sector W-59/02
Diplomatic Area, Off-Airport Road
PO Box 4090
Abu Dhabi
Tel: +971-2-4492700; Fax: +971-2-4444685
indiauae@emirates.net.ae; www.indembassyuae.org

United Kingdom
High Commission of India
India House
Aldwych
London WC2B 4NA
United Kingdom
Tel: +44-207-8368484; Fax: +44-207-8364331
fsvisa@hcilondon.net; www.hcilondon.net

Consulates in the United Kingdom

Birmingham
Consulate General of India, Birmingham
20 Augusta Street, Jewellery Quarter
Hockley
Birmingham B18 6JL
United Kingdom
Tel: +44-121-2122782; Fax: +44-121-2122786
cgi@congend.fsnet.co.uk; www.cgibirmingham.org

Edinburgh
Consulate General of India, Edinburgh
17 Rutland Square
Edinburgh EH1 2BB
United Kingdom
Tel: +44-131-2292144; Fax: +44-131-2292155
indianconsulate@btconnect.com; www.cgiedinburgh.org

United States of America

Embassy of India
2107 Massachusetts Avenue NW
Washington DC 20008
Tel: +1-202-9397000; Fax: +1-202-2654351
indembwash@indiagov.org

Consulates in the United States

New York
3 East 64th Street
New York
NY 10021
United States of America
Tel: +1-212-7740600; Fax: +1-212-8613788
hoc@indiacgny.org; www.indiacgny.org

Chicago
455 N Cityfront Plaza Drive
NBC Tower Building, Suite # 850
Chicago – 60611
United States of America
Tel: +1-312-595-04050410; Fax: +1-312-595-0416–7
hoc@indianconsulate.com; chicago.indianconsulate.com

San Francisco
540 Arguello Boulevard
San Francisco CA 94118
United States of America
Tel: +1-415-6680683, 6680662; Fax: +1-415-6682073
info@indianconsulate-sf.org; www.indianconsulate-sf.org

Venezuela

Embassy of India
Quinta Tagore, No. 12
Avenida San Carlos
La Floresta
Caracas
Venezuela
Tel: +58-212-2857887; Fax: +58-212-2865131
embindia-ps@unete.com.ve; www.embindia.org

Yugoslavia

Embassy of India
B06-07 Genex International Centre
Vladimira Popovica 6
11070 Belgrade
Yugoslavia
Tel: +381-11-2223306,3325; Fax: +381-11-2223357
indemb@eunet.yu

APPENDIX 4:
INDIAN BANKS

Indian private sector banks

AXIS Bank Ltd.: www.axisbank.com

Centurion Bank of Punjab Ltd.: www.centurionbop.co.in

City Union Bank Ltd.: www.cityunionbank.com

ICICI Bank Ltd.: www.icicibank.com

IndusInd Bank Ltd.: www.indusind.com

ING Vysya Bank Ltd.: www.ingvysyabank.com

Karnataka Bank Ltd.: www.ktkbankltd.com

Kotak Mahindra Bank Ltd.: www.kotak.com

SBI Commercial and International Bank Ltd.: www.sbici.com

Tamilnad Mercantile Bank Ltd.: www.tmb.in

The Bank of Rajasthan Ltd.: www.bankofrajasthan.com

The Dhanalakshmi Bank Ltd.: www.dhanbank.com

The Federal Bank Ltd.: www.federal-bank.com

The HDFC Bank Ltd.: www.hdfcbank.com

The Jammu & Kashmir Bank Ltd.: www.jammuandkashmirbank.com

The Karur Vysya Bank Ltd.: www.kvb.co.in

The Lakshmi Vilas Bank Ltd.: www.lvbank.com

Foreign banks operating in India

ABN AMRO Bank NV: www.abnamroindia.com

Abu Dhabi Commercial Bank Ltd.: www.adcbindia.com

American Express Bank Ltd.: www.amex.com

Arab Bangladesh Bank Ltd.: www.abbank.org

Bank Internasional Indonesia: www.biimum.com

Bank of America NA: www.bankofamerica.com

Bank of Bahrain & Kuwait BSC: www.bbkonline.com

Barclays Bank Plc: www.barcap.com

BNP PARIBAS: www.bnpparibas.co.in

Calyon Bank: www.ca-indosuez.com

Citibank NA: www.citibank.co.in

Deutsche Bank AG: www.db.com

J P Morgan Chase Bank, National Association: www.jpmorgan.com

Mashreqbank psc: www.mashreqbank.com

Oman International Bank S A O G: www.oiboman.com

Société Générale: www.sgcib.com

Standard Chartered Bank: www.standardchartered.com

State Bank of Mauritius Ltd.: www.sbmonline.com

The Bank of Nova Scotia: www.scotiabank.com

The Development Bank of Singapore Ltd. (DBS Bank Ltd.): www.dbs.com

The Hongkong & Shanghai Banking Corporation Ltd.: www.hsbc.co.in

Nationalized public sector banks

Allahabad Bank: www.allahabadbank.com

Andhra Bank: www.andhrabank-india.com

Bank of Baroda: www.bankofbaroda.com

Bank of India: www.bankofindia.com

Bank of Maharashtra: www.maharashtrabank.com

Canara Bank: www.canbankindia.com

Central Bank of India: www.centralbankofindia.co.in

Corporation Bank: www.corpbank.com

Dena Bank: www.denabank.com

Indian Bank: www.indian-bank.com

Indian Overseas Bank: www.iob.com

Industrial Development Bank of India (IDBI): www.idbi.com

Oriental Bank of Commerce: www.obcindia.com

Punjab & Sind Bank: www.psbindia.com

Punjab National Bank: www.pnbindia.com

State Bank of India: www.statebankofindia.com

Syndicate Bank: www.syndicatebank.com

UCO Bank: www.ucobank.com

Union Bank of India: www.unionbankofindia.com

United Bank of India: www.unitedbankofindia.com

Vijaya Bank: www.vijayabank.com

Associate banks of the State Bank of India

State Bank of Bikaner & Jaipur: www.sbbjbank.com

State Bank of Hyderabad: www.sbhyd.com

State Bank of Indore: www.indorebank.org

State Bank of Mysore: www.mysorebank.com

State Bank of Patiala: www.sbp.co.in

State Bank of Saurashtra: www.sbsbank.com

State Bank of Travancore: www.statebankoftravancore.com

APPENDIX 5:
PRIVATE HOSPITALS IN INDIA

Bangalore

Wockhardt Super Specialty Hospitals
154/9 Bannerghatta Rd, Bangalore- 560 076
Tel: 080-66214444, 22544444;
Emergencies and Ambulances: 080-66214101, 66214111
www.wockhardthospitals.net

Manipal Hospital, Airport Road, Bangalore-560017
Tel: 080-2502444
www.manipalhospital.org

Chennai

Apollo Hospital
21 Greams Lane, Off Greams Road
Chennai 600 006
Tel: 044-28293333, 28290200
www.apollohospitals.com

Hyderabad

Apollo Hospital
Jubilee Hills
Hyderabad – 500033
Tel: 040-23607777
www.apollohyderabad.com

Kolkata

Apollo Gleneagles Hospital
No. 58 Canal Circular Road
Kolkata – 700 054
Tel: 033-2585208, 2585217
www.apollogleneagles.com

Advanced Medical Research Institute (AMRI)
P-4+5 CIT Scheme-LXXII
Block-A, Gariahat Road (next to Dhakuria Bridge)
Kolkata – 700 029
Tel: 033-24612626; Emergency and Ambulances: 033-65500000
www.amrihospital.com

Woodlands Medical Centre
8/5 Alipore Road, Kolkata 700 027
Tel: 033-24567075–89
www.woodlands-hosp.com

Mumbai

PD Hinduja National Hospital
Veer Savarkar Marg
Mahim
Mumbai 400 016
Tel: 022-24447000, 24449199, 24451515, 24452222
www.hindujahospital.com

Wockhardt Hospital
Mulund Goregaon Link Road
Mumbai 400078
Tel: 022-67994444; Emergency and Ambulances: 022-67994155
www.wockhardthospitals.net

Asian Heart Institute
Bandra Kurla Complex
Bandra East
Mumbai 400051
Tel: 022-56986666
www.ahirc.com

New Delhi and surrounding regions:

Indraprastha Apollo Hospitals
Sarita Vihar
Mathura Road
New Delhi – 110 076
Tel: 011-26925801 / 26925858;
Emergency and Ambulances: 011-26925900
www.apollohospdelhi.com

Fortis Hospital Noida
B-22, Sector-62
Noida-201301
Tel: 0120-2400444
www.fortishealthcare.com

Fortis Flt. Lt. Rajan Dhall Hospital
Sector B, Pocket 1
Aruna Asaf Ali Marg
Vasant Kunj
New Delhi- 110 070
Tel: 011-42776222; Emergency and Ambulances: 011-26927000
www.fortishealthcare.com

Escorts Heart Institute and Research Centre
Okhla Road
New Delhi – 110 025
Tel: 011-26825000, 26825001;
Emergency and Ambulances: 011-26825002, 011-26825003
www.ehirc.com

Fortis La Femme Center for Women (Women only hospital)
S-549 GK-II
New Delhi -110 049
Tel: 011-41045104; Emergency and Ambulances: 011-41045104
www.fortislafemme.com

Index

accommodation (see housing)
Afghanistan 5, 7, 10, 22
airlines 100, 101, 112, 113
airports 90, 100, 101, 112
air travel 112
Akbar 11, 12
alcohol 12, 13, 46, 47
ambulance 51
Aryan 4, 5, 35
ATMs 40, 41, 42, 137, 139, 140, 177
autorickshaw 58, 104, 105, 196, 107, 108
Ayurveda 164, 165

bank accounts 141
bank holidays (see public holidays)
bank notes (see currency)
banks 137-142
bargaining 66
beggars 55
Bollywood 60
bribery (see corruption)
British 6, 13-16
Buddhism 28
building fund 171
bus 104, 105, 108
business 132
business hours 47

cable 152
car 102, 103
car registration 103, 104
car rental 103
Carnatic 62

cash machines (see ATMs)
caste 35
changing money 40
chats 79, 80
Christianity 27
cinemas 57
climate 36-38
colleges 171, 172
Congress Party 20
consultancy companies 131
corporate income tax 133
corruption 65, 66, 93
counselling 161
courts 38, 39
credit cards 42, 43
currency 40
customs 98, 99

debit cards 42,
dentist 162
deposit 147
discrimination 64
domestic servants 153, 154
Dravidian 35
driving 102
driving laws 102, 103
driving licence 102
driving test 102, 103
drugs 53
dependants 97

economy 39
education 167

electrical goods (also see household goods) 149, 155
electricity 45, 148, 151
emergency services 51
employment 114-119, 122
equal opportunity 123
ethnic divisions 34, 35
exchange rates 41
exit permit 175, 176, 178
expatriate society 59

fast food 79, 80
festivals 75, 76
food 77-85
fringe benefit tax 134
FRRO 91, 95-98
furniture (see household goods)

gas 151
gay and lesbian 53
geography 21
gods 30
graduate education 171
gyms 56

health 159-163
health insurance 163
Hindu gods 30, 31
Hinduism 27-30
hospital 159-161
household goods 149, 154, 155
housing 144-146

immigration, 86-97
income tax 125
Indian English 67-75
Indira Gandhi 19
insurance 44
internet 51, 152
internship/work experience 127
Islam 28

Jainism 28
Jawaharlal Nehru 19

languages 32, 33, 34, 53
laundry 46

Mahatma Gandhi 17, 19
maps 52
media 24, 63, 64
medical tourism 165, 166
mobile phones 49-51
money 137, 138
motor bikes 104
movies 59
Mughal 11-14,
music 60-63

networking 135
newspapers 63, 64, 115, 153
nuclear 20

opticians 162

Pakistan 4, 12, 18, 19, 20, 27
paise 40
Permanent Account Number (PAN) 125-127, 143
personal loans 143
pharmacies 162
police 51, 52, 90-93
police registration 91-93
political divisions 25
political parties 24
post office 42, 43, 177, 178
press (see media)
proof of address 142
proof of ID 142
property 156-158
public holidays 127
public transport 54

Rajiv Gandhi 20
recruitment 114
red tape 130
religion 26
rent 146, 147
reservation 168
residence permit 95, 96
restaurants 57, 58, 80, 81, 87
restricted permits 98
religion 26
Regional Transport Office (RTO) 102, 103
rupees 40, 41

safety 55, 111
salary 122
Sanskrit 4, 35
schools 169-171
shipping goods 177, 178
shopping 45
Siddha 165
Sikhism 31, 32
social scene 56
spices 84, 85
sports 56
states 25, 26
sultanates 5, 8, 19
supermarkets 46
sweets 85

tax clearance certificate 176, 177
taxes 124, 133, 134
taxis 104, 105
telephones 48, 49, 153
television 45, 63, 64
temperatures 36-38
time 47
time difference 47, 48

trains 104, 105, 109-111
transport 104
travel agencies 113

Unani 165
union territories 25, 26
utilities 147, 148, 152

vaccinations 161
value added tax 133
Vedas 5
vegetarian 77- 81
visas 86-97, 175
volunteer 127, 128

water 44, 45, 148, 152
weapons 53
weather (see climate)
work environment 118-122
work permits 118
working hours 127

Zoroastrian 77